T0208882

Ghost Tracks

≈

A Collection

Kelly Hamilton

authorHOUSE°

AuthorHouse™
1663 Liberty Drive
Bloomington, IN 47403
www.authorhouse.com
Phone: 1 (800) 839-8640

Published by AuthorHouse 12/03/2015

ISBN: 978-1-5049-0383-7 (sc)
ISBN: 978-1-5049-0384-4 (e)

Library of Congress Control Number: 2015905773

To my cheerleaders in the peanut gallery for your undying encouragement and gracious critiques. Know that your support and friendships are warmly treasured. And, not to be forgotten, thank you for the never-ending wealth of inspiration Mr. Hawke. You know who you are.

No one ever told me that grief felt so like fear.
N.W. Clerk (C. S. Lewis), A Grief Observed

What is one to do with unfinished affection?
Two Letters

Contents

Poémes & Petítes

Short Stories & Prose

Poémes & Petites

Matter of Time

Turn my watch and see it run
Say goodbye to old days gone
Break the chains that bind me in
Throw the reigns to the sweeping wind

Free myself from others' thoughts
Proud of the battle I've nobly fought
Stir my soul to an epic peak
Find those things I desperately seek

Know that change is my best friend
Guised as fear that kept me penned
Bound no more to social will
My heart's desire, my mission to fill

Heed no myths the world dictates
Lies untouched on casted bait
True belief in my soul's call
Save my faith from a downward fall

Rise above and serve heart's need
Fly through skies that don't impede
Peace and power I know I'll find
Mind over matter, just a matter of time

Sir AhlBegone

There once was a knight Sir AhlBegone
Who had a thing for women's thongs
The problem was
His frustration because
Those knickers of yore were too long

Yet
Yet

Paper men contemplate their substance
Origami serpents
Slithering through island of sand amidst concrete city
Shallow women refuse to stop the bleeding
Playing the game
Nonexistent hearts command fates
As ancient stones weep
For children lost
Yet
Yet
Doves fly above in hopeful courtship

Mourning Wind

Early this morning I felt Autumn grin
Catching a ride on a hushed mourning wind
Gilded bronze time has come calling too soon
Summer gives way to a new harvest moon

Thinking through all of our lost falls gone by
Digging through closets for things to keep dry
Stopping to wonder if Winter I'll see
Master his craft since you walked out on me

Lady Grace Summer is closing her doors
Now I'm alone on these spiritless shores
Void is our world you so far left behind
Told me you loved me, my love kept me blind

Now that it's quiet, another day's done
Can't help but wonder how far you have gone
Autumn shuts Summer and Summer shuts Spring
I'm cast adrift on a hushed mourning wind

Essence departed through tears in my soul
We were not started before me you stole
Just as a ghost ship sneaks out of her slip
Skilled you let go when I loosened my grip

Up with your roaming I could not keep pace
Widows on walks and I search for your face
Lone in my seeking your eyes I still find
Sometimes I still feel you touching my mind

Empty ice sorrow, my dark hollow time
Still feel your heart chiming rhythm with mine
See the sweet smile that you gave just to me
Realize you're gone and you've set yourself free

Chimneys will warm but my fires burn cold
Often I dream that you're still warm at home
Gone and set sail now you've caught the crosswind
I still hear your whisper, a hushed mourning wind

You cast me adrift on a hushed mourning wind
Drown in your whisper, your hushed mourning wind

Pen and Paper

always there
waiting to hear
my latest news
my newfound views

never do
i have to spare
any word
i need to share

i keep you near
to calm my fears
win or lose
you help me choose

Ledge

You've ruined me
complete and true
i'll never love
anyone but You

my standards set
too damn high
and now no one
can touch that Sky

You laugh at me
Your rule complete
You've always known
that You own me

i'm ruined now
beyond repair
no one will do
they can't compare

so as You laugh
and my arms stretch
i sway right here
on this tall ledge

Pastel

This child of moonlight
Absorbs her pastel mother
In great gratitude

Laws

the laws that enslave
the laws that set free
there's no way to know
what's required of me

I haven't been told
the rules are unclear
and so I must fold
to my deaf and dumb ear

expected to guess
from two different ways
the answer is hid
yet I'm told to behave

beaten and broken
loved and held tight
the words are unspoken
I cannot do right

from outside my window
I hear the wind call
yet inside my door
upon grace do I fall

the sky it entices
I feel its blue hope
then self sacrifices
and slips down that slope

darkness engages
I look for a light
where is the will
to trust and take flight?

which door to open
my choice is right there
my voice has not woken
I neither can bear

Whisper

Awaken to that breezy touch
Skin tingling, heart content
Between dream and wake

Beautiful pain

We are but a whisper apart
Imagine

Fire
Water
Earth
Sky

Imagine
Nothing exists but what we are

Beautiful torture

Drift now back in and down
Skin tingling, heart content
Between dream and wake

The Girl's So Sad

The girl's so sad every now and then
But she doesn't let it show
She keeps herself discretely hidden
So the world will never know
that
Sometimes she thinks she wants to try
Sometimes she thinks she wants to cry
Sometimes she thinks she wants to fly
Sometimes she thinks she wants to die

She just can't place the sense she feels
It's nothing in particular
But her blue suspicions nudge her mind
And she wants someone to fix her

She hears the mean stark fear that calls
Succumbs to its hollowing will
Out of the cold hard night it strikes
So fast her heart it chills

It leaves its rip so deep and wide
Too far for her to cross
Yet she swims against its high sharp tide
Tumbled and trembling and tossed

She keeps her heart well masked with effort

So the world sees only a smile

She's become a well-trained expert

At pretending for a while

When she wants to give up

Something keeps her going

'Cause she knows that she can't

Lose hope without knowing

The reason she's here

Her purpose and meaning

There has to be something

She's just not believing

Through her days she silently withers

But the icy world can't see

And through her lonely nights she shivers

In the dream of resting free

The girl's so sad every now and then

But she'll never let it show

She keeps her hopeful true-self hidden

So the world will never know

that

Sometimes she tries

Sometimes she cries

Sometimes she flies

and sometimes she dies

She'll Be Dancin'

Tonight the problems go away
Tonight the tears don't flow
On this night the dancin' calls
And trouble's on the go

She'll be showin' every other one
She's got the smooth right moves
Gonna break 'em all so way far out
Gonna show 'em all who's who
'Cause tonight this lonely little girl
Ain't got a thing to lose

For now the pain and soul-full fear
Are waitin' back at home
She knows they're sitting silent there
But for tonight, she's not alone

Maybe she should feel the pain
Just let it all cry out
But that'll take a lot o' time
So tonight she's goin' out

Now she dances by herself
She used to sway with him
They used to smile together
At the moonlight on their skin

Not looking for another man
That ship sailed long ago
But tonight for just an hour or two
She's gonna let pain go

Tonight she's got it goin' on
Gonna shake the heartache out
Gonna leave it back at her front door
'Cause tonight she's goin' out

And 'til the break of dawn
She'll be dancin'
So 'til the break of dawn
She'll be dancin'

Is It Worth It?

Tomorrow's promise
Because it is tomorrow's
Will never arrive

Four-leaf Clover

I found a four-leaf clover
Tiny as can be
Through miracle was placed just there
For tiny little me

I looked and looked to find one
Never to succeed
Then when I wasn't looking
It sprouted just for me

The wish that I want most
Is for you to come and see
How sad I've been without you
Now that we're not we

So with this sprig I ask you
Come back please don't you flee
Since I've been blessed with clover
Four-leafed not only three

Hero

Tattered and torn
Sword cast aside
The wound of the hero
Lies out and inside
It stealthily gnaws
Dark bruise on his shadow
His burden is heavy
On dusk field o' fallow
He suffers in quiet
He utters no word
His heart seeks to hear
What cannot be heard
Time has no meaning
Alone in his plight
His soul begs to soar
But fears to take flight
Desperate and lonely
He bows to the pain
Now native to him
A long gone-by friend
His throe is his comfort
So feel it he will
For he'd rather feel pain
Than forget how to heal
This is the wound
The hero must bear
To know that he's fought
And that no one is there

Red Walnuts

Red walnuts
Blue butterflies
Black trees in dreams
Save for my witness
Imagined it seems
No longer I question
Their uncommon truth
Belief's not been left
Behind in my youth

Pretend

You remember me in haunts
I never go away
Make up all the lies you want
But in your heart I stay

You think you've quickly moved along
But still you'll always know
That even though you think you're gone
My words play soft and low

Pretend and smile and use your will
Your heart you try to fool
To think that someone else can fill
Your needs the way I do

Alone with thoughts and writing pen
You see the smiles we shared
It's to my ghost that you give in
Right next to her in bed

You know there's no replacing me
With anyone but me
And you turn and look at her right there
But it's still my eyes you see

It's me your arms reach out to hold
When the midnight hour comes
And it's me whose kiss makes yours just right
Yet you think that you've gone on

Go ahead and blame on me
But you're the one who's wrong
You think that you are finally free
But on me your mind stays long

Pretend and think you will convince
What happened was my fault
But you know damn well it's you who quit
Deciding words you'd halt

You struggle hard and think you've won
But your mind just won't let go
You think that if you write it down
Your memories will not show

You tell yourself that you have fled
But know you can't forget
The sweet things that we always said
Are secrets not regrets

You see my face when you don't look
And your heart falls at the sight
Your soul is what your words forsook
But you still keep up the fight

Even though you say you're not
Ever coming back
It's my touch you always hear
Following in your tracks

You know it's in your heart I'll be
From me you cannot hide
And you know your mind will never be
Too far away from mine

In the day pride shakes its fist
And your will it leads the way
But in the night you feel my call
And your heart gives in and sways

You know that you'll come back to me
When your pride has run its course
And it's still me who haunts your heart
When the night is back in force

Pretend and smile and think you're done
But our truth won't go away
You can't let go, our soul is one
No matter what you say

Seagulls Fly

Where seagulls fly beneath me
And God speaks ancient ways
Rolling waves beseech me:
"Collect the dues you've paid"

Freedom beckons and a new life calls
Let the old one slip with the sun as it falls
Memories echo as water on shore
Winds carry means unheard of before

The tide is turning
This time it's real
Hope fills my heart
As finally I heal

Hope Lies

Hope lies with skill, it speaks in untruths
it lies in stealth wait for signs of its proof
Its phantom black secret has two distinct faces
it vacillates hot between both inky places

Its promises made, hope lies to the heart
I knew mine was lost from the very first start
I wouldn't admit it, I hid from the thought
that my caged soul could be so easily caught

I know I'm alone, your covert best secret
You destined me bound and then swore me to keep it
I'm out of your sight and I'm out of my mind
I know your sin secret, you need to know mine

Time's been so lost since I fell for your ways
I tried to ignore it, to wish it away
Your grip is tight iron, like Marley's long chains
Pulling me down into motionless pain

My secret low-lying, well-hidden and silent
beneath the debris I've piled up beside it
I covered my tracks as best as I could
but it came crawling back, we both knew it would

A host of confusions I've lived with for you
But never the savior I wished would come through
Indifference is bliss but elusive to me
If I could just catch it I'd finally be free

I played my drawn hand, on table it laid
My heart cried its breaking, my soul was afraid
The last thing that's left for these teared eyes to see
Is how far and fast you'll fly running from me

Hope lies divided, ornately décored
This hope holds fast tight, it won't be ignored
That one of these days as you look down on me
The one thing you're missing is what you will see

Hope is the shackle that keeps me bound here
It's all that I dream of and all that I fear
Without that grey ghost I'd fade from all sight
Into its heartless impenetrable night

The Passing

In angry sleep where virtue dies
I will dream no more
Their spirit sings and so I follow
A breath through slumber's door

Relinquish kingdom foul obtained
Ignoble prize possessed
Nay the promised godsend thought
Misuse I've not confessed

From hubris will my stained soul flees
Life at end unraveled
Perhaps fate's drifting arrogance
My soul no more will travel

World too vile from whence I come
My honor laid in waste
'neath closing gate my body steals
My shame trails in disgrace

Stolen glimpse I dare to take
Soft whispers I now hear
From good souls who have softly wed
Not spoken for my ears

Will I succeed in my last quest
Fool those that guard the sacred
Unnoticed traitor in their midst
A coward undetected

he/she

he heightened head
splashed sea
pushed problems past
evaporated in exposed beguiling blue

she shrugged silent
walked water
shining swimming steps
back to the dark black depths

have you ever noticed

have you ever noticed
the Sadness in poets
often outweighs
their better off days

the Humor is there
but cannot compare
to the pain and the fear
that's always right there

the Darkness does come
a prevalent one
ever so black
with pen they fight back

Tragedy's friend
in hearts it does live
seldom in secret
the poet must give

yet there are times
when Roots run too deep
so the poets' dim tale
inside they must keep

have you ever noticed

ever with kindness
except when in Anger
subject beware
the poet's a strangler

in well thought out lines
to themselves they are true
there's nothing as humble
as the poets' Haiku

sometimes their words
just can't find a home
Miscellaneous bound
with a toss of a stone

Heart on worn sleeves
rampant affection
the words are fine-sifted
a dusting confection

spirit Enlightened
heart nearly explodes
only through pen
can they fly within prose

tight knit quatrains
and constraints of the rhyme
the poet writes Forms
and counts rhythmic lines

in great gratitude
of Nature they write
expressing its grace
through words of insight

so lonely their Angst
with keen fine-tuned words
they still give their thanks
with penned lessons learned

when Fantasy dreams
they close tired eyes
and let it spring forth
bound by no ties

with pen they express
words bursting so bright
thank god they've been blessed
with Open Mic night

Literal Man

He's swept me away
With his words
He's written me out of his life
It only took one mistake
And he remembered her
I didn't know
What he meant when he said
Sweeping changes are to be made
I should have known right then
He's never minced or wasted words
He's a literal man
I can tell by the words he writes
Because they're no longer for me
He writes for her
No more for me
He's a literal man
And he writes for her
I never knew he had that much love to give

Lamb & Lion

When lamb lies down with lion
Night stills, world softens
In shielding comfort, hearts unhurried
Each repose in trust, content
The Universe responds in kind
And only a cricket sounds
When lamb lies down with lion

While You Smile

Hear my sad heart sigh
Under my mad sky
Feels my whole lifelong
I've heard your willful song

Sang for someone else
While
On my knees I knelt

Crying soul seeks peace
Trying heart will cease
Mind will not uphold
Threatens to unfold

Don't know why you chose
You
Left me in the prose

See the tears I cry
Under my mad sky
Took from me my heart
Then tore it all apart

Left me as you do
Smile
It I now see through

Hope's a borrowed word
Smiles to me unheard
Pain on me you pile

Yet all the
While
     You
          Smile

Choose

Infinite
Limited
Fast
Slow
Flexible and unforgiving
Found and lost
Respected and mistreated
Given and stolen
Discarded and treasured
Shared and hoarded
Honored and abused
Understood and misread
Past, present and future
Choices
Count them as they go
But waste not one
Choose
Or defer to Time itself

Such An Unhappy Man

Such an unhappy man
So lost
In grief's vacuum
The blackest hole in the night sky
Where dense pain resides in its home
The pinpoint of his universe
Does enough strength remain
To once again
Claw out of the cosmic debris
Swarming around and through
Every galaxy that ever was
Is there a savior?
Does he want one?
In the far reaches of his hope
Will he allow belief?
Unhappy is such a small word

A Friend of Mine

A friend of mine went home yesterday
He came for a visit, decided to stay
He stood by my side when I couldn't cope
He turned heavy stones to find my lost hope

Quick with his laughter through thick and through thin
His heart was wide open and shone from within
He rose high above each test that he faced
And did it with love, compassion and grace

He blessed me with wisdom and helped me with pain
He taught me the courage to fight my disdain
We'd celebrate sun on our big-engined bikes
Commiserate rain when it just had to strike

On eagle's great wings he took his last flight
He topped babbling brooks and flew to new heights
He rose above treetops and into moonbeams
He passed all his pain, crossed into his dreams

He left me a person with love in her heart
I learned of true kindness because of his part
On swift Ocean Breeze he sailed free away
The best friend I had he went home yesterday

Prison

Sun please don't come out today
With your light in your prism
I can't face your hope this way
It's quiet here in prison

If you insist and show your face
I'll never find the courage
To sink into my darkest place
And leave behind this knowledge

So stay behind the clouds today
And leave me in my peace
No reason for my soul to stay
In a heart that is deceased

Steeled

Black cat stalking prey
Suspended Grecian statue
Patience incarnate

Flow Through Me

I'm searching for connection
I'm feeling in the dark
I try to touch the source of me
I'm peeling off the bark

I'm quitting self-protection
Leave all my veils behind
The darkest ego of my youth
Its cruel strong shell that binds

Close my eyes and try to find
Knowledge of my truth
Strain for daylight, fight for air
No need to have the proof

Loving is its own reward
I've seen it do its work
Sweet miracles are hard at play
They help heal all the hurt

Somewhere deep inside me
I know that it's still there
When I connect it stills me
Recalls why I am here

The peaceful calm of certainty
The soothing of the soul
That's why we crave connection
It renders us as whole

When angels' grace flows through me
I give what I got back
I feel its warming comfort
Get me back on track

Trees Outside My Window

the trees outside my window
glow sunrise in my room
late fall this year still lingers
in red and orange plume

memories dreamt but not yet lived
though still forever pined
brought forth without remembrance
on melancholy shine

empty room, empty shell
the quiet fills my eyes
empty walls, empty bed
where fall forever hides

Prickly Pear

Prickly Pear passion
Fatally flavored fruit
Sensual succulent sinner
Pulling Pandora's pain
And Adam's affliction
Through thistled thirst
Relentlessly

Blue Mist

Ambling through forest, a blue mist begins
I'm struck by its beauty, the power within
I think of my loved ones who've gone on before
They step from my memory to greet me once more

I see Grandma and Grandpa and Dad's mother too
Bathed in soft sunlight on new morning dew
They've come here to tell me I'm not all alone
To share the pure magic that's waiting at home

Lost friends join in, I laugh "Merci beaucoup"
My cousins stride toward me devotedly true
My own mother comes through the silk mist and sun
She's gathered together for me everyone

I can touch them and hold them and feel on my cheek
Their kisses of kindness whose loss left me weak
There's my cat and my bird and my faithful dog too
My curly-haired poodle, I called her Chew-Choo

My aunt teases uncle for jokes he still hails
The light in their eyes tell the whole awesome tale
They shimmer with knowledge through overjoyed tears
How love transcends time and all space and all fears

The cheer that they bring me, the gleam in their eyes
Helps further convince me that life is a prize
So I'll walk through this day knowing they're by my side
And I'll do it with patience, grace, kindness and pride

'Cause I no longer doubt that I'm never alone
That they're all waiting there to welcome me home
Where forever we'll stroll as we've done so before
In that forest of blue mist and sun-dappled floor

Mountain Keep

On this mountain stood my keep
Now ashes and fractured hard clay
I must repair the damage you reaped
So mortared thick brick I lay

Black knight you came from relic past
My moat you sailed and crossed
Sweeping in so hard and fast
I'm left the ruin you wrought

Your breach so deep so dark so wide
It's further than I can see
There's nowhere left for me to hide
I strain on bended knee

You stole my heart, my mind, my soul
My defense has gone amiss
The wind now blows in hard and cold
And deepens my vast abyss

You battered and broke my fortified walls
My heart so easily caught
You ran into my unlit halls
In breadth and with no thought

My keep, my moat I now rebuild
Razed low like ancient ruins
Their fissures now must be refilled
Such speed you fast flew in

So scars I dam with brick I lay
To mend my walls again
And guard to fend without delay
My mountain keep domain

Blue-eyed Sailor

Blue-eyed sailor

Thin as a rail

First R&R!

Pressed whites

Spiffy

Bright-eyed and bushy-tailed

Innocent

Missing mom

Off the ship

Or gangplank?

You Knew

I think you knew when
you'd bravely go through it
I think you knew then
you wouldn't undo it

Your smile said goodbye
its truth was unclear
the shine in your eyes
no trace of stark fear

your face bathed in light
shone its contentment
your next turn in sight
your peaceful acceptance

To me quite unknown
the plan you had pondered
Your eyes did not show
the plot you had conjured

You already knew
our final look told
your word in your eyes
said my hand you'd still hold

Big Black Bag

The Tinman got a heart
The Lion got some courage
The Scarecrow got a brain
And Dorothy got discouraged

I know how Dorothy feels
though I tried my very best
That big black bag is empty
For me it's just a jest

I know that I can be
Complete all by myself
Alone and yet not lonely
Content up on my shelf

Don't know who I'm kiddin'
Our Dorothy she got burned
I'm tired of being lonely
It's gotta be my turn

Screw the big black bag
A victim me no more
I'll fight for what I want
I'm stronger than before

Dorothy was a wimp
Afraid of Wicked Witch
She turned into a gimp
She shoulda shot that bitch

I'm happy for the Tinman
I'm happy for the Lion
I'm happy for the Scarecrow
So I guess I'll keep on tryin'

The big black bag is empty
But not for long, you bet
I'm gonna keep on lookin'
And I'm ready with my net

Anyone

Is there anyone
Who can help my heart
Is there anyone
Who can dry my tears
Is there anyone
Who can let me trust
Is there anyone
Who can make me laugh
Is there anyone
Who can touch my mind
Is there anyone
Who can feel my soul
Is there anyone
Anywhere?

Summer

The soft sounds of summer, the smell of cut grass
Old mowers and prop planes near distant and passed
Steal flowers and berries from neighbors' back yards
Ain't nothin' right now that looks too gall darn hard

'Round young dads and moms we run humorous rings
Big brothers small sisters keep fighting 'bout things
Play tag and old Simon and Redlight-Greenlight
Then Hide-And-Go-Seek and make new kites take flight

We make up our games and we run in one place
A look and a glance then an all-knowing face
So strange are the words that "it's gotta get done"
These are the things that make high summer fun

Fix dusty old mitts and make baseball bats crack
Scream out at our friends "hey! lay down some tracks!"
Steal second and third and hear yells from the crowd
Slide into home plate and make moms and dads proud

Swing high over sand and lie quiet in shade
Then set up a stand and sell tart lemonade
We build us a fort and read worn out ol' books
While eating some pies baked by mighty fine cooks

Throw rocks at some bottles and don't keep the score
We smash 'em all up and look harder for more
We see who can best climb up old faithful trees
Scoot home to fix banged arms and tender scraped knees

Run barefoot through mud and muck up our moms' floors
Sneak thru the back door and skip out on our chores
Hear dads call out names but we're already gone
These are the things that make high summer fun

Draw pictures with clouds and trace where they have been
Then figure they're on their way home once again
Snooze under a tree and hide in the tall grass
Chase butterflies and big bugs and catch them in glass

Hear crickets and locusts, chase moths that take flight
Ditch bats and mosquitos that swoop in and bite
A cat on the prowl and a dog barks somewhere
No care we could think of will take us from here

Eat melons and cherries and peaches and cream
Stalk skippers and tadpoles and fish in the stream
No time for hard work, we think only of play
That time will soon come 'cause we don't have a say

No limits, no boundaries, just flowers in bloom
Magnolias and moonbeams, air scented perfume
Sleep sound in our beds when this golden day's done
These are the things that make high summer fun

Don't know what's to come and we couldn't care less
No plans and no worries, no thing we'll confess
Gaze up at the stars and the moon in the sky
They make us each wonder and ask of them why

For now come and sit by the creekside with me
We'll ponder our dreams in a cool reverie
When time is forgotten by infinite sun
These are the things that make high summer fun

Feeling the Squeeze

God please send her money
She just can't compete
With prices they charge
Her coffers deplete

They can't be refilled
Without help from you
So please in all haste
Do what you do

worry

you say don't worry
i say i don't know how
you say you don't
i say how
you say there's nothing to be done
i say i'd rather know
you say it's worthless
i say it's not
you do not suffer
i do

Here Am I

Someday you will find me
Floating in the sunshine
My heart beating
From a low flowing cloud
You will hear me call you
Singing through the rays
Sweet and clear
Come to me, I am here, come to me
If you look, you will find me
Where sky kisses sea
Where mountain meets valley
Where tide becomes ocean
Where rain quenches desert
Here am I, your sacred island
Here am I, your sheltering cavern
Here am I, your steadfast sail
Here am I, your solacing chalice
Come to me, Come to me
Here am I, Come to me

Sky
Sea
You
Me

Now What?

One plate
One fork
One knife
One spoon
One glass
Washed
Dried
Stored
Done
Silence
Everything in its place
For no one to see
Everything in its place
For no one but me
Now what?

How Many Hands

Whose is this face
In this old tintype picture
Fallen from grace
There holding his scripture

Did someone once love him?
Did someone once care?
In picture that's dimmed
His face was once fair

How many hands
Has this photo passed through
Discarded by clan
Yet once was brand new

What did he do
To be so forgotten
For strangers to view
as novelty item?

Will I too be left
In thrift store dust bin
Discarded no less
By uncaring kin?

I'll Carry You

I'll carry you for as long as I can
I'll carry you in these two small hands

I'll do my best to hear your call
I'll do my best to catch your fall

It was not I who guided you here
It was not I who made you fear

But if I can help I'm pleased to do it
If I can help to see you through it

I'm here to see if you come by
I'm here to heed your tearful cry

I'll wait for you 'fore turning the corner
Not leave you alone on that cold and dark border

I'll wait for you to make your choice
To follow, to leave, or use your own voice

I hope someday I can send you along
I hope someday you'll learn to be strong

But until that day I'll carry your past
And until that day I'll carry you fast

Unforgiven

So sorry
So sorrow-full
I stabbed relentlessly
And without knowledge
I pierced something sacred
Its sanctity
And I jabbed until
I got
Something I thought I wanted
How easily I would give it back
How I pray I could
How I plead with you
I beg for one word
One spoken word
But please God
not Goodbye
I slowly perish
One silent moment at a time
Am I to forever be unforgiven?
still begging
for one word
But please God
not Goodbye

Gettin' Old

Gettin' old can really suck
But with a bit o' Irish luck
Ripe old age might still just find me
Not in diapers and able to pee

When I wake up, I'm already tired
I find my birthday suit needs to be ironed
I can't see squat without my glasses
Now I know what a pain in the ass is

Escaping sounds from who knows where
I turn around to see who's there
Expectin' to see a croakin' ol' frog
No one's there, so I blame the dog

In mornin's mirror the person I see
Ain't the one went to bed with me
That person's old and creased and confused
I'm still young and smooth and unused

Too much time usin' the tweezers
God Almighty, what an old geezer
Hair's now growin' outta every orifice
Would it do any good to call David Horowitz?

The older I get, the more baffled I am
Ain't been so long since I did the cancan
The world puzzles me, I'm fully befuddled
Life's a strange game, I'm perfectly muddled

My joints are stiff and I can't do the Twist
Can't do the Monkey, can't make a fist
My body creaks, it won't stay calm
I threw my back out just puttin' pants on

My Snap Crackle Pop don't come in a bowl
It's just the back-talk from knees and elbows
My butt's done fallen and it can't get up
No telephone help-line for that to call up

Wherever you go, there you still are
So what if you got a few zig-zagged scars?
Wrinkles are charm lines, veins are road maps
You just gotta face 'em and let yourself laugh

I'll tell ya'll what though, it could be much worse
I could be layin' in the back of a hearse
The trick, you see, is learnin' to love it
So I'll take what I got and be gall darn glad of it

Timing

I thought it might be timing
I thought you'd feel the same
I thought that if I waited
you'd listen to your shame

I lied in my unkowing
that years would fly on by
and never did I see it
that fall would rule my sky

Time is so unsettled
Shifts, stands still and flies
ahead now life has hurried
Sped 'way on skylark's cries

I look back now to witness
my folly that's been played
I didn't see your punchline
But saw my trust mislaid

Today I am but counting
the minutes as they pass
Hoping that your timing
toils kind and true and fast

sands

sands of time
sand castles
black and white beaches
sand in a bottle

eon
neon
trees on

tear down the neon
for a place to put trees on
return our sands
forever to eon

Hawk's Play

Spied hawks play about sparrows' slate wings
Made puppy dance and old cat purr
Stalked feather's descent behind dove's startled flight
Flattered eyes with flowering stems
Absorbed sundown and sang barley's breeze
Inhaled peach and picked another
Heard silence and tasted sunlight
Touched fields and fall's warmth
Crested summit and perched in seclusion
When my pardon comes, I will parry with Hawk's Play

Candle

half-moon high
wind whips outside
sun begins ascension
another day
to fill with thoughts
full thoughts of empty things
how to make sense of nothing that looked like something
exhausting thoughts
lonely thoughts
yet there's color in the sky
clouds to hold it
hills to welcome it
trees to breathe it
birds to ride it
gossamer wind veils and guards the endless well
that threatens to swallow
one misplaced gust
and she will be gone
for now
the wind keeps her afloat
carries her weighty thoughts
the candle burns low
consumes her hollow hopes
dreams of nothing
one misplaced gust
and she will be gone
and another sun will ascend

Wine Velvet

Curtain dowel above a door no longer there
Skeletal traces of things that used to be

Pictures and old records thought gone long ago
Wrapped in wine velvet with gold tassels

Unnecessary things left behind
Or kind reminders for the one who remains?

How Many

How many times
Must you make me beg
Just to hear your silence

How many times
Must I say I'm sorry
Just to ease your anger

How many times
Must I write you my tears
Just to see you blind

How many times
Must I plead
Just to win your laughter

How many times
Must I tell you I love you
Just to watch you turn away

How many times
Must I promise
Just to know your rejection

How many times
Must I miss your arms
Just to feel them around another

How many times
Must you answer
Just through infinity

Christmas Carol

We wish you a Merry Stressmas
We *wish* you a Merry Stressmas
We WISH you a Merry Stressmas
And a happy cashier

Consumer Machines

From pirates we feed
They eat up our dreams
There's too much to choose
Consumer machines

We bite and we chew
We chomp at the bit
We can't wait to buy
The rest of their shit

We can't get enough
We waste what we have
We throw it all out
Then more shit we grab

It ain't gonna change
Not anytime soon
We eat and we slurp
From their silver spoons

We buy this and that
Must have and must do
You talkin' ta me?
I'll take that one too

We follow the lies
Of rich and their greed
And so we don't hear
The Earth as She bleeds

We see what we've done
When at Her we look
Our Earth's on Her last
Precarious foot

Consumer Machines

We keep our eyes closed
Our heads in the sand
It's nice just to doze
And not give a damn

We buzz and we bang
Consumer machines
We better buck up
And quiet Her screams

Cause until we do
She's just gonna burn
And then it's too late
To know what we've learned

Melody

Melody, my sister
I ask your forgiveness
So ashamed I ridiculed
So humbled by your strength
I don't know where you are
Now my transgression I cannot confess
Gone, you are just gone, and I am afraid that you are cold

I Can Hear the Wind Talk

When you absorb me in your arms
I can hear the wind talk
It speaks in caresses
And in multi-languages
It whispers in brushes
And in every color
It screams in strokes
And in delicate textures
It sighs in touches
And in treasured memories
It laughs in tickles
And in feather-winged birdsong
And then it sleeps

Sentience

Your intensity has taken refuge behind creation
and is well hidden in its shadow
Pain has degraded you to inhabit a hovel
Instead of your castle
I do not know where you belong
You do not know where you belong
Your tears have been replaced by others less welcome
You have not been deafened
But you have been muted
So sadly, your Sampson & Delilah existence has been silenced
Passion, where has your sentience gone?

She Has No Name

Campfire light envelopes Her face
Black robes, silver-streaked black hair, grey eyes
An antique soul, She is of me, She is outside of me
Wise beyond the last galaxy, She is the core of mine

Always there, always has been
She reveals Herself to introduce me to Me
Offers Her knowledge
When I need it, when I seek it, when I can accept it

Wisely detached, but not always so
Ever so slightly smiles in spite of Herself
She is pleased to see me see Her
She knows I know, She knows I don't

Earthen clearing surrounds Her
Beyond circular forest, all shades of green, house Her little helpers
Smiling, they are happy in their occupations
Campfire light allows only glimpses

She guards my little multi-coloured creator
She guards my characters
Red, purple, green, blue
She guards us all, all of me

She is the truth, She holds mine
I am on Her dole, She regulates
From Her steadfast grounding
She is me, She is not

Behind....... Her gypsy wagon carries my necessities
my desires, my anger, my joy, my cravings, my power, my pain, my
jealousies, my lust, my connection, my passion, my love, My Lace
She shows me how to dance on My Lace

She is universal
She embodies all that ever was, that ever will be
She is the wind, She is the tide
She is the moon in all its phases

She is the gatekeeper, She is mine
She is the liberator, She is mine
She is the key, She offers pieces to me
When I need it, when I seek it, when I can accept it

Surrounding the forest, my atmospheres undulate
They are out, they are in, just like Her
She calls them when needed
She feeds them to me

She is the origin of my sparkle, my glow, my shine
She is music, She is mine
She always answers when I seek
When I work, She reveals miracles

She doesn't wonder, She doesn't need to
She has no need to forage, She has no need to gather
All is at Her fingertips for the plucking
Her coffer is filled, She has no poverties

In Her forest, in Mine
She just is, I just am
When She shows Me
When I dance on My Lace
I just am

She has no name
She doesn't need one
I have no name
I don't need one

In Our Forest
She Is Smiling

Fame

Her name is famous now
They've made her ageless now
And hold her blameless now
She's too predaceous now
Her values tasteless now
Her conduct graceless now
Her speech mendacious now
Her acts salacious now
Her crimes outrageous now
Her habits tameless now
No longer stainless now
Her blight contagious now
Her star is flameless now
They've made her faceless now
Her pride is baseless now
Her life is aimless now
Her soul is faithless now
Her face is nameless now
No longer famous now

Picket Fence

Picket fence
Weathered white
In the middle of nothing
Nowhere
Ancient two—story house
Battered and bruised
One—hinged gate
Now without purpose
Creaking in the wind
Slam
Creak
Slam
Creak
Stripped picket fence
Keeping nothing out
Only in
Eighteen white cranes
Perfect as snow
Stand unbending

What's a Wicket?

What's a Wicket you ask?

a chaser of toys
he's furry and white
he pounces on gophers
and gives them a fright

he begs for my food
and so loudly snores
he's bouncy and round-faced
and walks on all fours

he gives me that smile
that I can't refuse
he's funny and knows it
and quick to amuse

he's silly and smart
and sleeps all day long
he eats when he's hungry
and must tag along

he likes the fast wind
to blow in his face
with head out the window
he wins the car race

I just don't know what
I'd do without him
his sweet sparkling eyes
and big doggy grin

That's a Wicket.

Only One

Shifting blocks of memoires
Sealed
Immune to influence
Darkened with age
Black patina
Pieces of the puzzle

One more
Accommodating
Persuadable
Untarnished golden grain
Beautifully pristine
Precious
Seductive
Precarious
Dreadfully empty

A single pull on the iron ring
Will expend the last promise
A box to fill
And seal
And shift into place

One last gift
One last chance
Only one
To make sense of me

Stronger Than I

She hangs on for dear life
She hangs on for mine
She's all I have to sooth my soul
She's the one who won't let you go
She won't let me go
She begs you not to go
She's all I have
She knocks at your door
She waits
She cries
She steals herself
She knocks again
She cannot move past your doorstep
She will not
She refuses
She cannot let go of her belief
She does not give up
She will not let me
She has her own will
She is stronger than I
She is Hope
And when she dies
I will follow

Diamond and Coal

Love
Sincere Passionate
Undulates Fantasizes Protects
Rapture Kindness Kill Rupture
Undermines Falsifies Perpetrates
Stealthy Painful
Hate

Silent Sounds

You speak in songs
You whisper your want
But never my name
In your silent sounds
I hear heavenly words
Yet you talk in tales
To write your wrongs
And pretend on paper
That you do not yearn
That no one and nothing
Can separate our souls
I am your precious passion
And you are the heart of my heart

Spring

the seed of love planted
blue air in the spring
high hopes upon branches
do waver and cling
bright flowers in glasses
in windows they gleam
two hearts filled with gladness
that flutters on wings
thoughts hold no fastness
and run in wide rings
heads full of madness
when love arrows sting
souls free of sadness
small looks swiftly bring
shy smiles are both anxious
for what love next will bring

Kingdom Gone

Yesterday a swallowtail
Took rest on azure flower
Ever bright in lucent power
Nestled in his bright green bower

Fifteen, twenty years it's been
Perfection in his finest
"Hello", I whispered to his shyness
"It's good to see Your Highness"

Breathing here is hard for you
I'm shamed for what we've done
Fevered heat beats from our sun
So to your home you rarely come

I'm glad you stopped, your time is short
Take flight, be on your way
Alight somewhere with calmer days
Away from this exhausting haze

Flutter by and soothe my soul
And bless me with your hue
The only thing I ask of you
Please tell your friends to stop here too

Was Only

I thought it was a chair in the moonlight
But it was only a reflection in the glass
So I watched the moon disappear
Knowing it was only the earth turning

I thought it was comfort in a cradle
But it was only a reflection of our truth
So I watched your silhouette disappear
Knowing it was only my thoughts burning

Forces

You remind me of a past that is no longer mine
With the dawn that is rising
Clouds cover the sky telling me that I need to stay away
And bow to the forecast that has brought me here
Only to live in ghost rhymes
I can now give to the forces
That have delivered me to a new past
Being made by welcoming others

Barricade

Devouring, unquenchable Demon demands
Crone stirs sinuous supplements into her brew
For the chainman who has chosen her

In shadowed shack
Where crows crouch in corners
And Light dares only muted murmurs
Through silent stolen Sunday glances
From behind my barricade
Worriedly watching in only swift glimpses
In fear for my future

She mixes mortar for mortals
To stifle their souls
And gratify her greedy God

Snapshots

Solo snapshots
Of solitary self-shadows
Standing stalwart
Where sorrow seams with survival
In singular synergy

Words as a Weapon

Come to me child
And take these old hands
You're feeling defiled
And I understand

I see in your tears
My life inside yours
And inside your fears
I've dwelt there before

In battle against
The shadows that threaten
Your will may relent
But never do question

Trust in your soul
For you have the power
To keep yourself whole
With grace and with valour

Fight for your heart
Don't ever surrender
Your strength is your guard
Protection forever

Words convey more
Than brute ever could
So keep them in store
And be understood

Life is a lesson
We live and we learn
But words as a weapon
Give phrase a good turn

Pong

Trapped in a box
                              Bouncing off walls
        Looking for sleep
                        Stolen by pen
        Angry at time for running

                      Angry at mine for stealing mine
No sense in fighting it
                        Nothing left to do but hope
        That there will be enough

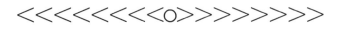

Valentine's Day

Valentine's Day sucks.

The End

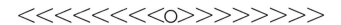

She Rises

Today she doesn't want to try
Today she wants to stay in bed
And not even try
Today she sees the sun rise
And doesn't know how it can
One step at a time

He rises
In his happy future
Light-hearted
In no effort
Touching another as he does
Her ghost left behind
In the quiet dreams
Of a past that he no longer needs

She rises
From her happy past
Heavy weighted
In great effort
With no one to touch
His ghost haunts still
In the tearful dreams
Under that sky that used to be hers

She draws herself up
She knows she has to try
Because if she doesn't today
She won't tomorrow either
So she cries
Today she doesn't even want to try

But she will
Because maybe today
She will take one more step

You Didn't Run

You didn't run away, you got away
You needed to go because you'd been abused for too long
So young, only sixteen
So wise to get out
You have no fear, you're saving yourself
I'm so sorry I didn't love you enough
If I had known I would have tried to help
I know I can help you now
Though you know I don't have enough and that's ok with you
So you're gonna get in that car and go
Because you must save yourself
You're not running
You're getting out
Oh the relief I feel
For you to be on your way to freedom
I'll remember you for as long as I can
I hope it's forever
I smile when I see you be driven away
To a place where you'll be safe
At first I cry for me
And then I smile for you
Be free
Live well
Find safety in the love of others
So far away
Oh
So far out of sight
And you get smaller and smaller
I'm happy now that you will be safe
And loved
Wherever it is that you're going
Gone now
Out of sight
But still in my heart
In the memory of you

The Artist's Studio

Dead plants
Dusty counters
Dust-bunnied carpet
Empty refrigerator
Bulletin board walls
Dried up air fresheners
Dirty dishes
Overflowing laundry
Unmade bed
Dead flies between window panes
Full ashtray
Glass-ringed desk
Tattered chair
Out-dated photos
Hungry dog
Angry cat
Only the Art
Merits attention

Downstream

Hope is carried downstream
on the back of a tear
Faith imitates
they flow easily without struggle
the host resigns
helpless
and they are gone without a whisper

New Dentist

Oh joy oh joy I found a new dentist
To my delight she's not an apprentice
A prick with her needle
Does not make me feeble
Or jerk up my arms in defenses

Hooray hooray the pain is now minimal
She's not one of those who you would call criminal
She makes no assault
Cuz her hands have no fault
And plus my chair's fun cuz it's spin-able

Whoopee whoopee a smile on my face
When leaving her office in happy quick pace
Though smile is quite crooked
With face looking stupid
At least I don't leave in disgrace

Huzzah huzzah the victory is mine
A thing of beauty, the rarest of finds
But you get what you pay for
and I have to save more
Cuz now in my bills I'm behind

Angry Eruptions

Intermittent with pitched darkness
That hovers in quiet wait
Wills in combat
I speak to the rages
Volatile volcanos
Angry eruptions
Tear the black apart
With red fire
And molten wrath
Shadow submits
But only until
It is his time again
To smother

Just A Little Wish

Star light star bright
First star I see tonight
I wish for me
I wish for others
Love and peace
For this world's troubles

Beautiful Stranger

Ah beautiful stranger
I should seek shelter at the thought of you
Fly from my heart
Hide from my passion
I should flee from the first silken word uttered through your lips
Take flight
Run toward destines unknown
I should blind my eyes at the sight of you
Turn my attention
Ignore my desire
And yet to you I am drawn like steel to magnet
Hard
Fast
Absolute
Beautiful stranger
Where do you go?

No Need To Try

Through fate you found me
No need to try
You leave me stranded
Without a goodbye

You pull me out
To play like a trinket
But I don't think
You ever think it

I die every time
You reach for my hand
A toy on your shelf
Is all that I am

I follow your shadows
And keep in my distance
If ever they see
You're gone in an instant

Your kiss lingers still
On my lips as you turn
I just don't think
That I'll ever learn

You say you don't love me
But I know you feel strong
You think you're right
But I think you're wrong

The words you utter
They shatter my soul
But you ignore love
And she'd better know

The Welcoming of Home

As I Forgive Others
So I Forgive Myself
Then Mortal Disappears
And I Touch the Welcoming of Home

twelve twelve twelve

twelve twelve twelve
how to commemorate?

but of the twenty first?
will the world incinerate?

should i believe
what those would propagate?

trust what they say
and so well disseminate?

just give in
and truly anticipate?

i best get moving
time to proliferate

and write this poem
so hard to contemplate

try to decide
the words to generate

my fruitful mind
i cannot infiltrate

they got me now
i just can't concentrate

i must write fast
and quickly circulate

for my fellow poets
to deftly deliberate

so on twelve twelve twelve
this poem i'll terminate

One Step Forward, Two Steps Back

I was doing well
I was doing better
Then only one thought
Made me remember

One step forward
Two steps back
I can't seem to find
To make my way back

Each day I fight
To keep you from me
Sometimes I earn
A blank memory

I pray every night
A new dawn will bring
The cleansing of you
The smite of your sting

But today nothing matters
Success is not mine
My final goodbye
I just cannot find

Wind

Demanding
Welcoming
Piercing
Caressing
Burning
Cooling
Cutting

Biting Stinging Blinding Sweeping Comforting
Tingling Clearing Cleansing Calming
Freezing
Warming
Damaging
Healing
Screaming
Whispering

Wind

Fire

I'll never lose my fire for you
It will burn forever
It doesn't matter what you do
You know we're best together

Your cutting words will never change
This fire inside of me
I know you'll never rearrange
Your world to be with me

And yet this fire will always burn
It's out of my control
Just admit what you have learned
It's me you want to hold

In these flames that mesmerize
You see me standing there
It's my face you've memorized
Pretending not to care

It's you my fire is burning for
These flames can't pierce your shadow
And they can't make you not ignore
They'll never have that power

This fire burns hot and goes up higher
It's yours that joins with mine
It's built from our seared souls on fire
No kindle left behind

No other love has ever been
Or ever will be born
Equal to what we both know
Is ours and ours alone

The Vanity of Youth

The vanity of youth
Manifests with age
It rears up its head
Shameful lost sage

Unwelcome wisdom
Known long ago
Ignored at the time
But neglected for show

Aware of the lessons
But back turned in pride
If only I'd listened
Instead chose to hide

Temptations too great
For such a young fool
So now wisdom rides
In a dark dirty pool

Wisdom is meant
To comfort and sooth
But its purpose is lost
In the vanity of youth

THE CURE FOR JEALOUSY

DISAPPOINTMENT CANNOT HIDE
IN A MAZE OF HIGH-HEDGED DREAMS
COMPARISON IS THE ENEMY
AND FALSELY IS PERCEIVED
TO DISMISS INEQUALITY
IS THE CURE FOR JEALOUSY
AND GAINING SIGHT OF WHO TO BE
IS THE PRIZE FOR VICTORY

Nowhere Left

How can I move on when I waited so long for you to come?
How can I forget when every moment of my life is a memory of you?
When every thought I have I want to tell you?
When every sight I see I want to show you?
When every word I hear reminds me of something we've said?
When every dream I ever dream or have ever dreamt is of you with me?
When everything I am or ever was or ever could be is yours?
When your name is my Sky and your soul is my Universe?
How can I move on?
There is nowhere left to go.

Corner Woman

I saw a woman yesterday
Standing on a corner
Had to be 'bout sixty
Maybe even older

Clean old clothes and thinning hair
With quaking sign, "Please Help"
I stopped to hear her story
And the hand that she'd been dealt

I offered her the well-used bill
She took my hand in hers
"I pray that God will bless you"
She smiled through shining tears

She told me she was stranded
Her car had broken down
She'd used up all her money
Just to get to town

"I'm a senior citizen",
She said through frightened eyes
"I didn't know just where to turn
Now God's sent His surprise"

"You're an angel darling,
He'll save a spot for you
Now I know that I'll get home
And pray that you will too"

I left her standing weightless there
With sign and in sad face
I wondered what was going on
And felt immense disgrace

The richest country in the world
Our children cry to sleep
Shame and anger, helplessness
Engulf me 'til I weep

When will this damn chaos end?
This horror we've allowed
A government too selfish
To see we're no more proud

The egos high up on that Hill
Take all and think it's theirs
Won't they ever realize
They're stealing from our heirs?

We must stand up and heed the call
They won't stop 'til we make 'em
The times, yessir, they're clearly here
But they sure as hell ain't changin'

We can't afford to go to work
And we can't afford not to
They must be held accountable
And do what they damn ought to

Return our pride
Return our health
Return us to our land of wealth

Of Magic and Men

Forgotten episodes
Where only stones remember
Their dead monster brethren
Memory pallbearers
Carry emaciated faith
To the drums of a rumbling dirge
Blind in their pilgrimage
On well-worn paths
Trodden through the ages
Old sins eternally reaping their burdens
Forever to be rebirthed

Elements

earth   where sustenance is gifted
air   where freedom thrives
fire   where sin is cleansed
water   where life is born

Hidden

where is that promise

the one you gave

to me

I've been waiting

to claim that promise

in deed

where have you hidden

those words you spoke

so sweet

there on your lips

I heard a promise

for me

there in your eyes

I saw your promise

so deep

it's not from me

your promise hides

I see

Hidden

you left that promise

behind you, before me

to keep

it lies in my arms

your promise inside

of me

I hold it here

for safekeeping

it weeps

your promise lies

to my heart, through my soul

I bleed

will you look? will you seek?

for those words you gave to me?

I plead

will you find? Will you speak?

will you break? Will you keep?

or flee

I'll wait for you

to find your promise

in me

your promise

hidden from you

but not from me

not hidden from me

I Give Up

You look me right in the eye
And scornfully tell me you don't believe me
Then you scream at me saying you always knew it
Make up your mind!
PICK one for God's sake!
You've got me spinning in circles
yes no yes no
And no matter what
wrong wrong wrong wrong
you look at me with such contempt
then want to be friends
I can't keep up with your anger anymore
I give up
God how liberating
When I give up

Wake Time

Oh Happy Crafter
What joy that you have risen from your deep slumber
For my quill to feast on your multi-coloured countenance
So quick now in your wake time
I cannot keep pace
Each thought
Each word
Each vision
Desires birth
Desires release
Yearns to BE
Almost devious in your disruption
But oh so welcome
I am thankful to surrender sleep
For I am no longer alone

Deliver Me

Deliver me unto my dreams
Far from this outside prison
Where fear is coarsely visceral
And makes its deep incision

Where truth is brutal and rapes the senses
And cries are never heard
I've fallen short of my defenses
To this harsh and hollow world

Deliver me to my inside realm
Into extinguished time
Mirrored in another star
Where heart and soul still rhyme

Deliver me from this icy world
Harsh and bright and broken
Where granted prayers in silent thought
Never need be spoken

Never without when I am within
Cocooned from angry peering
Deliver me into song's womb
My home of cosmic clearing

Let me return
And leave me be
With peace of heart
Deliver me

The Last Step

The height needed to fly
The climb to get there
Throughout the struggle knowing

that the last step

    off the top

        will be the steepest

Grandfather to Grandson

there will be times
when you are confused
but if you try
mistakes can be used

think before
then make your choice
use your heart
then use your voice

an honest sorry
goes a long way
regrets are only
mistakes that we've made

there is a cost
more often than not
but better to pay
than lose the whole lot

so hold your head high
boy of my heart
it's ok to cry
then make a new start

Without Restrain

Teardrops on a windowpane
Where fear and hope blend to make pain
Crossing all boundaries without restrain
Impossible from which the soul can refrain
For is there anything as darkly inflamed
As a love so deep that it's gone insane

Asya's Farewell

Friends must part
With tears and smiles
Bittersweet
Farewells, long miles

Sep'rate roads
So sad it seems
High hopes for
Each other's dreams

Sure to meet
Again one day
Parting's not
The final say

River Rat

You're lazy and boring
You don't have a friend
Ain't one who likes you
It's us you offend

Well lemme just say
That I can relate
Been told all those things
More often of late

But you know what I do?
It's more I appall
And have much more fun
When I crawl up that wall

I hang on those curtains
In homes I've invaded
And I know for darn certain
My tail's been paraded

I crawl up that wall
And I get in those cupboards
if they're stupid enough
to leave 'em uncovered

Been swung at with brooms
But I'm quick as a cat
Been damn near harpooned
So at them I spat

I hissed and I snorted
Through challenging smile
And for show I contorted
With gleeful high-style

I'm a Rat of the River
And I'm happy to be
Cuz I make'em all shiver
And run under their knees

Been plenty o' times
They don't see me there
But most o' the time
I give'em my stare

I even laugh shrill
High-pitch they can't hear
They don't have a clue
How closely I peer

When they're fast asleep
I take my revenge
At their kids do I peep
Through cradles tight-hinged

Some they may say
I'm a nasty ol' soul
But you know what I do?
I give 'em what for

It's them with the issues
They ain't mine no-how
So I take to their tissues
And in them I plow

So here's what I say
My kindred rat friend
There's more just like you
You DO have a friend

How Can?

How can one instant be agony and bliss?
How can this love possibly exist?

How can one hope be so dichotomous?
How can one soul be both full and damn bottomless?

How can one faith both sing and cry tears?
How can one moment be triumph and fear?

How can one mind think such disparate thoughts?
How can one spirit soar yet be caught?

How can one heart fall again and again?
How can one body carry the pain?

How can one vow be so defiant?
How can one will be so compliant?

How can one wish be frail and insistent?
How can this love be so damn persistent?

How can one endure?
How can one survive?
How can one be two
and keep itself alive?

These Tears

These tears are different
These are for you
These are in thanks
To the heavens above
For helping you feel
I am joyous at the sight
Finally
I know I was right
Finally
Your words tell me I was right
And now, each tear has found its purpose

The Climb Is More Difficult Than The Fall

∞

Unconditional Love

↑

Peace

↑

Forgiveness

↑

Compassion

↑

Acceptance

↑

Understanding

↑

THE CLIMB

~

THE FALL

↓

Frustration

↓

Hatred ~ Anger ~ Jealousy

↓

Pain

↓

Fear

Ψ

Ghost Tracks

Choosing memories to leave behind

Carried by ghost tracks throughout my mind

Dismissing the sorrows and keeping the rest

Cherish the ones when I was my best

Kind-hearted gestures in past I have made

Will be the ones allowed not to fade

Pain and sadness on ghost tracks will walk

Out of my heart and into the fog

There to be swallowed and hurt me no more

My ghost tracks of memories will walk past the shore

Short Stories & Prose

Aficionado

It is born of helplessness and breeds Itself. It is not the pain, grief, sorrow, and emptiness from the loss of a loved one. It is not the same because It is open-ended. There is no concrete evidence for Its existence. Yet It has form and It is visible. It is Its own entity.

It fills all sight and is immune to light. It is dichotomous in Its void abundance. It is a dense hollowness that carries Its own unique weight. A physical heaviness from which there is no escape. It covers the whole body and It smothers the heart. A dark and consuming fog that suffocates. Its gravity is stronger than this earth's. It locks Its quarry down with Its thick mass that immobilizes with numbing fear and renders the body into a state of physical shock. Anesthetized agony. It overtakes hope and leaves Its victim speechless. Sightless. Staring eyes with no vision. It allows no thought to penetrate the murk with which It has covered the mind. No future thought, no past thought, no present thought. It is crippling. It does not cease.

It is unrelenting in Its search for Its next satisfaction. It lurks and never strays. It waits in ambush hovering just outside and watches for Its cue to assault, that moment between sleep and wake when dreams are still real. That quiet bridge that evolves peace into precious disappointment before all-encompassing fear takes hold. That moment the victim holds on to so tightly for one more second just to forestall the inevitability of Its return; the victim's last feeble defense against Its attack. It lives for that moment right between forgotten and remembered. Knowing that disappointment is the lesser of two evils that the victim prizes, it relishes its destruction. And when the time is ripe, It teases Its victim out of exhausted sleep with dreams of respite, allowing only a solitary treasured second of happiness and peace of heart. Its mark is helpless to combat Its craze. And when the fear explodes, Its immense gratification is realized. It stabs with Its reality as It cackles at the foolishness of hope. It is evilly gleeful to wrench pain and fear into the body of Its host. Its arsenal of weapons is limitless and every victory feeds It. It has no worthy rivals. It does not fight fair. It delights in any attempt at defense because It knows It will conquer. It waits in anticipation of Its host's next futile effort to escape and then self-congratulates upon Its triumph. It invades relentlessly and does not let go. It has never known defeat. It needs no rest and It does not die.

It hates the living except for the tears It waits to consume. It allows only one gasp and then absorbs the breath as energy. It doesn't need the air but It likes to play. It steals oxygen and exhales toxin. It ages and atrophies Its prey devouring one cell at a time. It is a parasite. It is barbaric. It is a perpetrator of the soul.

It is proud to show Its face and is always on the offensive. Blow after blow, It deals Its damage with precision. Its strength is effortless. It expands and contracts to wring out more tears, more anguish, more fear. Ever pressing, ever pushing, It celebrates the succumbing of the will. It laughs at struggle and then tightens Its grip. It squeezes to the point of breaking then releases only to keep Its host alive. Constrict and release, constrict and release. It chokes and lets go. It crushes and revives. Against It there is no aegis. There is no recourse. It has no mercy. It is uncaring save for Its own existence. It revels in agony and It thrives on pain. And the more pain It creates, the stronger It becomes. It is gleeful that the word 'despair' cannot rise to Its power. It laughs at the term 'worry'. It is the unyielding, overpowering, omnipresent, and omnipotent fear of loss. It is the Aficionado of the Unknown. And It is a psychopath.

Train of Thought

Train of thought. Who thought of trains? I think, therefore I am. I am Spartacus. Sparks don't cuss. Cuz I want to. Wanna dance? Dancing in the moonlight. This little light of mine. Mind over matter. It doesn't matter. Doesn't that hurt? Hurtful words. Words are not for keeping. Keep this confidential. Confidence in you. You don't mind? Mind your manners. Miss Manners. Misinterpret. Pretty highly rated. Rated G for everyone. Everyone talk at once whydontcha? Talk is cheap. Get it cheap here! Here's your hat, what's your hurry? Hurry along. Long live the king. King Kong. Conga line. Railway line. Trains. Train of thought.

The Pelicans and the Pervert

On a typical day, I faced what I consider two of the most extreme emotions within a nanosecond of each other. Joy and fear. Most of us tend to think of these emotions as quite opposite, polar in fact. On this day, in me, they each produced exact motor responses: breath stopping at the height of a gasp and immobility. One in awe, the other in terror.

◇◇◇◇◇◇◇◇◇◇◇◇◇◇◇◇◇◇◇◇◇◇◇◇◇◇◇◇◇◇◇◇◇◇◇◇◇

I went to my favorite beach one day (one day out of many beach days) to feel, hear, smell, and see the beauty, absorb the nurturing. When I was leaving the ocean, my mind of course was planning what I needed to do next - dump the sand out of my shoes, get gas, stop at the store, get home, note what I'd learned on this day.

I turned around to look out upon my favorite view in the whole wide world once again - atop a cliff with the ocean's expansion before me, rocks and sand and surf still there where I'd left them. Comforted, I turned. And saw them: pelicans. So big and graceful, flying so close at the cliff's edge that I could have touch them. I gasped in awe. In unadulterated, physical joy. My breath stopped completely. Looking past the leader, I saw that there were dozens of them. All following the same flight pattern, they seemed to be complying with instructions from their control tower. One after the other. Some solo, some pairs. So, so close. Their magnificence literally took my breath away. I was immobile. In that moment, in between my last breath and my lungs demanding fuel, there was a grand suspension, the world stopped, time ceased, it did not exist. I felt large and small at the same time. Their flight produced no sound, they did not speak. I did. The only semi-coherent utterances I was capable of was "whoa" and "holy shit". Everything else was in no identifiable language whatsoever. Finally, the anchor glided past. I swear he dipped in a little closer to me as if to say "Farewell". I watched them all go, still flying on their invisible path. My heart began to beat. I hadn't noticed it had stopped. As they receded into the distance, another movement caught my eye. A car. Speeding into the narrow and deserted parking area. Faster than necessary, unsafe even. It pulled up directly behind my truck. A man. "What a dick", I thought, "speeding in such a confined space. There's plenty of room here, why park within a foot behind *me*?" Under my breath now I repeated: "dick". Returning to packing my beach gear away, my mind slipped to the pelicans again. "Wow. Coolest thing ever." Then it kicked in. Caught gear. Wait a minute, this isn't right. This is very, very wrong. That was not just fast and stupid. That was aggression. That was anger. A wave of evil intent washed over me. And then the absolute knowledge of it. Fast intake of breath, then it stopped completely.

The sluggish gears in my brain began to clasp the speeding cogs of my body, and it was screaming: MOVE!!! MOVE!!! Taking hold now, the void between my mind and body filled with CODE RED!! I dropped everything. Literally and figuratively. I dropped my beach stuff. I dropped the thought of getting the sand out of my shoes. My mind kicked off plan-mode and fastened onto my body's flight-mode. It said, "Get to safety! Get in the truck! Lock the doors!" The relative shelter of the secured doors enabled me to concede to the immobility produced by the after-rush of adrenaline. I felt my body go to code orange. My heart began to beat. I hadn't noticed it had stopped. I was still except for the return of my breath. After a minute or two, I began to notice that I could move. But now I was *pissed*. "Who the hell do you think you are?" Rational thought returned to the backseat as defense shifted toward offense. "*Fuck* you, I'm not leavin'." (The thought that he could have had a weapon never crossed my mind until this writing.) I watched and I waited. I felt his aggression turn into frustration swiftly followed by anger. I heard him start his car. He whipped around mine and sped out of the lot. Fast and furious. Pissed and palpable. Asshole.

Relief set in, and I began to comprehend what a close call it really was. It made me sick to my stomach and brought tears to my eyes. My body shook and I deepened my breath to calm it. I closed my eyes to allow myself to fully feel all that had just transpired. I knew this was rare. I knew this was important. I searched for the words to verbalize the intensity of this experience, the antiquity of my emotions: so primal, so limbic, so raw; to express the wonder of it all: so extreme, so divergent, so polar. The pelicans. The pervert. Back to back. Joy and fear. Peace and terror. Identical intensity. I found equal gratitude for both. I appreciated their separateness and I marveled at the connection between them as evidenced by my body's matching reactions. I pondered the link's significance. I nurtured the knowledge of that non-space. That suspension of time. I had found the words I sought.

Finally, (fifteen minutes? thirty? I'm not sure) I began to return to the world. It morphed through my sight and the rest of my bodily senses. All its beauty. All its threats. I realized that this time I had been immobilized through pure thought. I found my physicality again. My body moved and I open my eyes. In a minute or two, my mind returned to its tasking duties: "Gotta dump the sand out of my shoes, get gas, stop at the store, get home, note what I've learned on this day". As I finished packing up my gear, my thoughts returned to my experience. I finessed its epiphany. On autopilot, I started my truck, pulled out of the parking lot, headed toward the gas station. A few minutes down the road, as I caught glimpses of the ocean's views, I realized that I'd never gotten the sand outta my shoes. I laughed.

Black Gold

Through closed eyes, she feels him hear her. This much hasn't changed. Unlike before, she sees his back toward her, turning a blind eye to what he knows is true. He tries to ignore the tears calling to him, yet their persistence does not allow the burial of their plea. Sitting there, not listening, but hearing just the same. Her tears make their unwanted entrance into his thoughts and slither down to constrict his throat. The tightness there incites their crotaline travel to his heart. Like a drill that sprouts Black Gold, shame draws them up to his own eyes. So unkind, so vicious, the words he spoke to cause them. He didn't know he was capable of such cruelty. She didn't either, though she should have. She turned a blind eye too, and so they discover a new common ground.

The Runner

The Runner easily jogs as he watches the competitor give chase. He snickers with glee at the effort the competitor makes. He is winning, and he has no need to watch where he's going, so he keeps a laughing eye on the competitor. Oh, how joyful. How happy he is. He's winning as he always does. He feels so unstoppable, so superior. This is a piece of cake. He doesn't know the name of the competitor. Why should he care who this joker is? Why does this guy think he can beat me anyway? Didn't anybody tell him I never lose? Didn't anybody ever tell him that I always sail right through everything? Jeeze, what a loser. I'm not even breakin' a sweat.

In his inattention to what lays ahead, The Runner Hits The Wall.

Exploding mortar and sharp-edged brick assail his body as he instinctively takes the fetal position to protect himself from the shrapnel. Every inch of his body is attacked. Head, face, shoulders, arms, hands, back, ribs, legs, feet. Trapped. Stunned. Immobile. Terrified. He's been given the reprieve from full burial. Or perhaps the punishment of sight. The Runner has no time to decide which as he frantically tries to dislodge himself. He can't find a way out. He sees the debris piled upon him and feels the aftermath still raining down, but he can't get a purchase on anything. He can see it, he can feel it, he can touch it, but when he thinks he has a hold on something his hands pass right through. Ghost hands. He is no longer snickering. He is hysterical. His back is up against the wall and he cannot move. He steals a glance at the space that used to be behind him but now is in front. His fear builds as the competitor fast gains ground. His mind is in a tailspin. The Runner is not laughing anymore. All glee has left his countenance. Who IS this guy? What's his name? Why am I so afraid?! Why can't I get up?! I'm not hurt, I can feel my arms and legs, but I can't get these bricks off me. The Runner's eyes dart between the competitor and his own cagey, elusive entrapment. All the while furiously trying to get himself free. He is shocked at the competitor's speed. He has learned that The Competitor is no joker.

He looks down at his entanglement. Up at The Competitor. Closer now. Down, up. Closer. Down. Desperately searching for freedom. Up. Frantically tracking The Competitor's progress. He sees The Competitor slow his pace to stride easily toward him. Down, up. Here. The Competitor is here. The runner's double-edged horror rips through his body. He recoils in his fear that is now physical. Pain has found him.

The Competitor is expressionless, soundless. The runner can only hear his own whimpers. He is terrified of The Competitor's presence. He is terrified of The Competitor's *EXISTENCE*. Head bowed in fear-induced protection, the runner slowly and uncontrollably raises his eyes toward The Competitor's face. Now the runner sees. He recognizes The Competitor for his dominance. For his supremacy. He recognizes The Nemesis he never understood he had, but who has always been there. Now. Now. Now he understands. It is The Competitor who is unstoppable. It is The Competitor who is superior.

And in the runner's terrible, knowledge-filled exposure, he cries The Competitor's Name. TIME.

False Hope

False Hope. Alive. Dead. Filled streets. Now empty. Life
abounds. Now quiet. A dream. So real. Reality's silence.
Stark awakening surprises and befuddles, stupefies the
soul that was soaring moments before. Crippled now.
Still. Succumbing to the inevitable. The impenetrable fog
of despair. Vulnerable. Greater Hopelessness perches in
a tree like a bird of prey. Waiting for the perfect moment
to strike. Searching for the wounded one. The weakened
one. Ravenous, insatiable. Ever patient. Ever watching.
Anticipating. Knowing. Focused. Narrowed eyes declare:
"I am the King of False Hope.
That mouse is mine."

I Dreamt You Finally Saw

I was leading you toward a beautiful place that I knew existed. That I know exists. A place I'd found for us long, long ago that I've waited to show you. That I've told you about. A place you'd never seen but knew was there. That you know is there. Where you've wanted to go. I finally knew you wanted to go. I know still, you want to go. You know still, you want to go.

You followed with curiosity and an "I'm game" attitude on your face. In your eyes. In your smile. Over a route of ugliness we walked along a run-down street void of people. Deserted industrial buildings with broken windows rose to heights unseen. Menacing concrete. In their threat of oppression, they were bending toward each other. Growing together high, high above our heads. I ignored them. You didn't care they were there at all. You didn't even feel them watching. We walked through debris twirling and falling again in chilled gusts of wind that attempted to assault our faces and bodies. Chaosed wind. I promised it was there and it would get better. Wait 'til you see it. Anticipation picked up my pace. You smiled at my excitement.

We reached a threshold, where concrete ugliness began to taper off, to give way to the beauty that awaited. To the beauty I knew was there. I know is there. Within our sight was its promise. A small creek riding through dark green trees and bright feathery ferns. Their canopy offered welcoming shelter for our journey. The foliage seemed to be parted just for us. For our passage only. Its presence beckoned. Its promise had been waiting.

Something heavy, concrete, stood in the way of easy access. In the middle of the creek it stood in impenetrable anger. In intelligent challenge. In scathing mock. A remnant of the ugliness we had withstood to get here. It held fast, anchored, as if it had placed itself there of its own free will.

I saw her then. She was following behind you, just out of sight, but I ignored her. You didn't care she was there at all. You didn't even feel her watching. You were not hiding me. You were not hiding you. You were not hiding who we are together.

I felt your soul. I knew you could go no further. My heart broke for you. Your heart broke for me. Our heart breaks for us. I knew we would never reach this place of freedom that we both wanted. Want. We would never reach the promise given. I suffered with you the well-hidden sorrow you finally acknowledged knowing that we could go no further together. You saw what we both wanted. You finally saw its existence. But you knew you could not pass the barrier. You wanted to, but you knew you could not. We stared in lost hope at the trail to that place we both desired. Needed. Need. We stared at the path leading to our home. And as one we saw our unattainable destiny. And our hearts fell. Together our hearts fell.

But she was there waiting to catch yours.

For Frank

We arrive here as infants and as we learn to toddle, we begin to feel the weight meant for each of us to carry. We do our best to bear each additional ounce delivered upon us. And we fall from that weight and we use our strength to stand back up again. As we learn to keep our balance, we learn to walk. We stumble over and over again. We struggle. And then we learn to run. We run and run. And some of us run too hard. Too fast. All the while accepting more of the weight meant for us and us alone. And our knees buckle, and our muscles burn. And yet we run and we hold the weight and sometimes, when we fall, we just don't have the strength to get back up again. We love you buddy, and we'll celebrate you always, as you always celebrated us.

Close the Doors
(a meditation)

Softly close the doors to this world
To this country
To this state
To this county
To this town
To this street
To this building
To this room

Leaving only you within good company
Safe within this room
Safe within this gathering
Comfortable
Peaceful
Calm

Ready now to welcome change
To move on with what's next for you
Grateful for times spent and saved
Memories will fondly remain
And now it's time for Happy Closures
New adventures and exciting beginnings

Close the Doors

Preparing now to return to this room
Consistently safe and comforting
Touch that enthusiasm for something new
And bring it with you

As you come back

And open the doors

To this room
To this building
To this street
To this town
To this county
To this state
To this country
To this world

Far Too Long

Hope hangs her head in matured innocence. The battle for her belief lost. Long ago promises now shadows of their former selves, visible only to these few whom ever knew of their existence. She and her protectors, her defenders. Pain stands nearby in heavy breath, always her champion. In continued aegis, he turns toward Fear behind him and recognizes the countenance of one who has accepted his fate. Anger sparks out of sheer will, determined not to relinquish his true nature. From one to the other, Compassion administers consolation like a healing salve to repair wounds under secured bandages. Overlooking the carnage, Faith keeps each in sight as mother with child.
Perfected guardians all.
They wait.
They watch.
Sentinels at their posts.
Hope lifts her head, so small yet still strong, and listens for the next.
The wait seems far too long.

Her Majesty

At a time when I had first dramatically changed the direction of my life, I was suffering from doubts about my decision. I had taken a huge leap of faith and was feeling the gravity. Uncertainty was creeping into my heart frequently, and I was feeling very unsure of myself. What if I'm wrong? If I fail, how am I going to support myself? Is the risk of my desire worth it? Is this what I'm supposed to be doing? All these fears were flying around me like wasps on a watermelon.

I decided to spend some time at the ocean, soak up some sun and surf. She always soothes my soul, and I knew she would help me today.

I arrived at the beach I've been visiting all my life and took in the view from the cliff above. Beautiful as ever, but I could see that the surf was quite high. Well, a little water ain't gonna stop me, so I gathered my "beach-backpack" and headed down the trail. Some say you have to be a mountain goat to get down it, but I think a little lamb would do quite well.

I knew that the remnants of a storm from New Zealand was hitting the coast, and I wanted to witness it. My beach is small, and limited by large rocks I can traverse to get to the next beach over on either side. Though confined, there's plenty of room for a few families to enjoy. Today, I was wonderfully alone. The waves were bigger than I'd ever seen before, crashing with a thunderous roar, engulfing a large flat-topped rock my parents used to use as our kitchen table. They were assaulting even the bigger ones we'd climb on as kids closer to the water's edge. I found a place I where thought I could hang out and stood there for a while, watching. I thought of my brother and how much he loved this place too. I knew he'd be amazed to see our beach in such a state, so I dug for my camera and waited for just the right waves to crash over our family dining table. It didn't take long, I was getting the rhythm of her rhyme and could time her tempest pretty well. I got a couple of great shots, marketable if I do say so myself, and stayed tuned into her beat a bit longer. The waves were cresting close, but I decided it was ok to settle down. I got all my paraphernalia set up just right and built my roost. (Man, I'm a pain in the butt. Why I have to carry everything I own everywhere I go, I'll never figure out.)

The day was brilliantly sunny, warm, and welcoming. I didn't dare close my eyes though, I knew I needed to keep a keen eye on'er. No napping today. Every now and then a wave would hit so close it made that carnival-ride thrill wash over me. I unloaded my work (yep, I bring my office with me too) and focused my attention on the task at hand. Working, watching, working, watching. As the focus of my work became sharper, my study of the ocean became just glances, though they were frequent and well-timed. Every now and then, I was reminded of what was happening around me when the cacophony of a particularly big wave made me jump. I'd check it out, then put my head back down. In heavy concentration now, I got this feeling. Something was tickling my gut. I looked up to the sea. She was still protesting her inconvenience, but was not out to get me yet. I resumed my place on the grindstone. Then it came again. That feeling. So strong and so sudden this time. Tenfold. My body tensed. Heat washed over me. Nerves moved from At-ease to Attention in a split second. Fear. I spun only my eyes to her this time. No other part of me would move. I watched her throw a couple more waves my way, but they sure weren't life-threatening. My logic was in combat with my intuition, but it could not overcome my instinct. On-edge, intuition and instinct conjoined, and it was screaming at me now. I could not look away. I went into blitz-mode. Cramming my stuff hither-dither into my backpack (if you knew me you'd know hither-dither is never an option), I kept one eye on what I was doing and one eye on Her Majesty. My fear rose to a fever pitch. I couldn't move fast enough. (Fleeting through my mind was the reminder of how high-maintenance I really am.)

As I grabbed up my towel, the biggest wave of the whole day hit. It was magnificent. The SECOND the last corner of my towel left the sand, the wave's backwash rushed up behind me. It came within one-half inch of where the towel had been just a nanosecond before. "HOLY MAMA that was close!!" I looked up to gage the distance between me and the trail and saw that the water had blocked my way back up. Three-feet of rushing, churning ocean water between me and my salvation. Knowing that what goes up must come down, I was nevertheless dumbstruck about what I should do next. Scale the cliff? Wait for the Coast Guard? Light a flair? What? I stood there still stunned as the water subsided. Much, much too slowly for me. But it did tiptoe its way back to its source, taking its own sweet time (I guess it wanted to stop and smell the roses...) Realizing this might be my last chance, I grabbed everything I had, packed or not, and ran, full-speed, to the trail's end. (You should'a seen me. I looked like I was looting through an obstacle course.) I made it half-way up that trail in record time. Carl Lewis would be jealous. I turned around to see where I'd been and stood there shaking from the adrenaline. When I could breathe, I whispered, "Jeeze Lou-eeze that was close". Any bigger and that bad boy woulda takin' me out.

I took one more adrenaline-heavy sigh then made my way up the rest of the trail. Reaching the summit, I once again took in the horizon. Stepping ever-so-closely to the cliff's edge, I peered down to my beach. The little piece of sand I so carefully selected was on its way to being gone. Even my shadow's shadow wouldn't fit there anymore.

This experience completely validated my intuition and my instincts. It answered the questions I had been asking myself, relieving the doubt I had been struggling with: Am I doing what I'm supposed to be doing? Is the risk worth it? Will I fail? It validated my belief in me. It strengthened my trust. I floated home on the liberation I had just been granted, and continued on my journey.

Parisian Stroll
An Image

Let the fog lift.......Slowly it dissipates until the view is filled with the dusting of a new light snow on a Parisian cobblestone side street. Victorian streetlamps softly illuminate the surroundings. Merchant windows display bright, multi-coloured lights advertising the goods inside their warm shops. Just there is the second-hand bookstore - a favorite haunt. And next door, for the eyes' feasting, an antique shop proudly showcasing its collection of Fabergé eggs. Inviting aromas of the many cafés and boulangeries scent the air with baking breads, brewing coffees and frosted cakes – an abundance of decadent delicacies found only in this small corner of the world.

Patrons in snug winter coats, sheltering hats, and warm gloves leisurely stroll as their booted footsteps echo off the cobblestones. Mingled in and behind, is the sound of cups and flatware clinking on china and citizenry conversations. Some loud and boisterous - big smiles and arms waving; others hushed and conspiratory – hands holding hands and eyes searching eyes above cozy bistro tables.

Slowly turning a corner, again the fog thickens. Sadly, it is time to return to the outside world. Circling back the way traveled, there is a knowledge that this place will soon be revisited to see the sights, taste the flavors, hear the sounds, and revel in the vibration of this little piece of heaven.....

Two Letters

~~~~~~~~~~~~~~~~~~~~~~~~~~~~

22 July

Dear Grandmother,

I pray this letter finds you well and enjoying steady good health. I write to you this time, Grandmother, because you have always afforded me your kind and patient ear, and I am in the depths of a despair so frightening that I fear for my sanity.

For many years you have allowed me to share with you the intricacies of my relationship with a certain Mr. Hawke, and now I ask you to listen to my account of the latest events in our relationship, for it has come to pass that along with the object of the deepest love I have ever felt, I have forever lost my closest companion too, and in such a manner that his treatment of me defies all conscionable behavior. He raged from my life suddenly with incomprehensively cruel words and without explanation. Yet my love for him persists to flow through my very blood alongside my indescribable grief only to be reinvigorated with each beat of my heart, its poison uncleansed. I have cried to exhaustion so often that I cannot imagine from where the tears continue to stream, for my soul has been left desolate. His exodus has marooned me with only my shattered heart as company for I am sure that his departure is definitive this time.

In fear of my deteriorating condition, I have turned to those few whom I trust in hope of their comfort, but their lives so busy with their families and affairs, they hold their time very precious and cannot spare me much. Perhaps it is that they feel helpless to console me because they have never been exposed to such pain, or if they have, they choose not to revisit their own in the perception of mine. In those who have tried with well intent, I have found that they have always been unable to understand the level of love I have for him and so, in turn, cannot comprehend the equally profound agony that consumes me now. I can ascertain by their comments that they think I am suffering the consequences of my weak will and I am quite embarrassed by their conclusion. None have ever understood how I could surrender my life to the love of a man who never returned my affection or how deviously my submission occurred. Through no fault of their own, they hold not the ability to truly conceive my plight or to simply listen without well-meant advice as to how I should extricate myself from my situation. They are helpless to offer me the kinship I so desperately need and are therefore restrained to only rewording their prior warnings and recommendations. Though their advice is tendered out of protection for me, their attempts to encourage me with their solutions only discount my steadfast pain. As I continue to seek release from my misery, I have experienced the humiliation of being reduced to beseeching their comfort. I hear their excuses for begging off a visit, and I have begun to doubt their value of my friendship. I feel they have tired of my plight and find my life's struggles too taxing, and, having come to feel as a burden, I am afraid to bother them more with my troubles for fear I will lose their friendship altogether. This discomfiture only widens the split in my heart and devalues my own belief in my character. I bear no ill will toward any, for I understand the difficulty of feeling virtually powerless to aid. All their counsels and recommendations I have given to myself many times over as these insights have always resided in my intellect, but my heart stays forever resolute in its unwillingness to accept its liberation afforded by these truths. Thus it is, Grandmother, I place my grief in your hands in the hope that you will listen to my story as you have for as many years as it has unfolded.

Before his leave-taking, every early morning I would leap from my bed in anticipation of what our meeting would bring. I greeted each day with joyful impatience to see his face and hear his voice, to see the promise in his smile as he said hello to me once more. Now every night when my mournful exhaustion demands rest, I fear falling asleep, for upon first consciousness when troubled slumber has passed, my elation lives for only the instant of a hummingbird's wing before the memory of the vacancy left by him jolts me out of my anticipation to plunge my soul deeper and further into the abyss than it did the day before, a place so dark that a glimpse of sunlight threatens to damage my physical body. I feel as if each morning's remembrance has become corporal and uses its newfound materialization to strike my heart into the crouching position of a beaten mongrel. Every time I remember he is gone, my soul is impaled by a new devastation and dark disappointment sinks my core so deeply that it burns, driving my soul ever further into that void where everything I knew disappears. And upon each awakening, I feel as if I am losing him all over again. My body lies frozen in a state of motionlessness as if enchained, forever bound by the weight of my hollow heart. I now have no notion of what to do with time for I am capable of naught save thinking of him. My mind is unclear and remains incapable of performing even the simplest of tasks, and when I need to make the slightest decision I stand dumbfounded for my thoughts are forever occupied with memories. How horribly idle are all the hours that used to be filled with his presence and no matter how earnestly I beg his image to release my mind it turns a deaf ear. He assaults my dreams without right and without abeyance and my thoughts of him do not cease throughout each day. I cannot control the recurrence of the many words he said to me through smiling eyes, each never failing to bring more tears to mine. He inhabits each waking moment and every sleepless dream. Everything I see, everything I hear, everything I think reminds me of him. The sound of a caller at my door causes my heart to race in glee of his arrival and electrifies my impatience to speak with him again. And just as suddenly I remember that my friend has deserted me, and my hollow spirit plunges once more into the bare space he has left behind, into that place where every thought wounds. Even writing these words, my mind turns to his image as I question if he hears me when I think of him. Why does he continue to torture me even after he has gone? I wonder, Grandmother, if I have become truly insane, for as I write my tears still flow with heavy longing to see his face. It makes me wonder how emptiness can carry such weight.

In effort to keep my heart from the pain of remembrance, I read and attempt progress on my needlepoint as distractions, but soon I find myself staring blindly out my window as my tears well through and my lack of *interest returns. Though I beg my relentless memories to leave me be they persist in their betrayal. I have no ambition for my gardening, and no longer does the promise of outings with friends entice me. I cannot take my beloved walks along the shore for it is there that I always remember our happiness. I must be in dire need to leave my room for in each place I am forced to go, I see our presence together and cannot bear the agony of the space he has left vacant. Even in my small quarters, every sight and sound remind me of him and renew my distress. The excitement of spending the day on horseback no longer lightens my soul, and I am ashamed for neglecting my equine friend and companion knowing that he needs to stretch his legs and feel the wind in his face from a healthy trot. When I do make my way to the stables to satisfy myself of his care, I see his head weighted down with the sadness generated by missing me. When he hears my boot steps he always gives me his delighted whinny, and I see the hope in his eyes that we will ride free once again. The disappointment in his face as I leave breaks my heart and doubles my guilt for remaining stationary. Even my writing has suffered, for it is now three months passed since the event and I have been unable to summon the will to take up pen, even to write to you. I have been afraid of involuntarily attracting the painful longing that I know will come as soon as I finally begin to speak of my condition, for it always results in uncontrollable tears that make me take to my bed again. I fear collecting the post, as I will once again be reminded of the absence of his letters, the thought of which makes me remember each conversation that ever took place between us. In my small parlor where my writing desk resides sits the chair he used to occupy during our visits, its emptiness now palpable. Only his letters that I have attempted to hide from myself keep it company, huddled in silent wait as if they possess malicious intent. Many times I have thought to destroy them but cannot bring myself to do so. The room confines the happiness we once shared and I cannot bear the lovely memories that room returns to mind, so I pass the door quickly without a glance to avoid another piercing of my heart. I am unable to sit at my desk to write, and I have not submitted one piece of work since April of this year because he took with him my inspiration and my greatest encourager. As I write this,*

I must steel my nerves to keep my pain at bay. I find reprieve in only my isolation so I stay in my room and have only the will to rise from my slumber and dress for the day, praying that on this day I will overcome the burden of my limbs to feel sunshine again, to speak to another soul. When I am forced to venture outside, I am embarrassed for all to see the circles under my eyes and my weighty countenance. They address me in kindness and inquire of my health, commenting in gentle concern that I appear tired. I find that as people greet me, the absence of speech has addled my mind so completely that my words are halting and barely comprehensible so I avert my eyes to evade our contact and to avoid making any new acquaintance. I see my body change for lack of exercise and nourishment and my movements are slow and calculated, for even my body falters sometimes in its unsteadiness. Oftentimes, Grandmother, my immobility causes me to feel as though someone could put to better use the space I inhabit. So most days I simply lie back down and pray for slumber to come to relieve my pain, but even in sleep my dreams conjure images of him disappearing from my sight.

Though you have heard it entailed time and again, never Grandmother have you failed to provide me with sage guidance or to be equally delighted in my joys as you were saddened by my heartaches, always without judgment. Though others find it difficult to comprehend my acceptance of the routine of Mr. Hawke's and my relationship, you have appreciated my long-lived quandary, never speaking with any words that were less than compassionate. How many times, Grandmother, have I written of my suffering when he left me for months at a time? And how many times have you shared my happiness at his return? My dearest Grandmother, I beg once again for your wise counsel to my most fervent question: WHY DID HE DO THIS?

As you well know, Mr. Hawke and I met at a time that one of his business ventures brought him to a local venue I often frequented. At our first meeting, we were immediately engrossed in a conversation that unveiled our common interests and we spoke until the function's end. Our attraction to each other's character proved to reveal our appreciation of the other's intellect as well as humor, and the next day he called on me to continue our discussion. I must admit to being happily surprised that he found my company intriguing, and the attention of such a stately man was seductively irresistible. Our rendezvous continued for many days until his work called him away, and even then, though I would not admit it, I knew that I was in danger of breaching the protection of my well-guarded heart. He continued to post letters to me quite frequently, but as his business kept him away, they tapered off until I heard no news at all. I was, of course, heartily disappointed, but after some time I went on with my life as I had before. Many months passed before he returned, and his contact with me renewed our acquaintance. Thus, our pattern began and has remained. Though I always attempted to renew my life as it had been before our reunions, I was so irresistibly fascinated with him that I could not refuse his continual request for my company upon his every reappearance. Each time he called on me only to leave for time indeterminable, my distress at his absence grew lengthier and more devastating and it became increasingly difficult to return to my individual life. Never once after he stopped his communication did I seek his company, for every time I knew that I needed to put an end to our relationship for my own protection and dignity. Twice, after months of his absence, I was able to disregard his multiple attempts to contact me, but his persistence lasted beyond my resolve. He is a man, Grandmother, whose account of himself does not allow refusal of any desire. How deviously my love for him grew. My need of his company occurred so gradually that without my knowledge I had relinquished to him every piece of me. So many times after his dismissal, I have endeavored to entertain suitors who have called on me for my company in the vain hope of leaving him in my past. But each time I involuntarily compared their qualities to his and found them lacking. I am convinced Grandmother, that my heart will never be free to love another, that my soul will forever be enchained by his ghostly purchase, for I continue to love him. How crestfallen and disheartened I have been each time he so easily set me aside and how ashamed I am that I was always so uncontrollably willing to welcome him back. With every disappearance, my devastation cut more deeply than the time before and my dignity withered even further, never to recover the ground it had lost.

Our relationship has carried on this way since our first encounter and has remained so throughout his worldly excursions during which he has continued to request my companionship whenever he has been in close proximity. In the course of our long relationship, we have had only transitory times together before he returned to his travels staying gone for months at a time. As in the beginning, after each departure he would continue our correspondence for a brief period until other concerns drew his attention and he once again afforded me no word of his well-being. Each time he returned, my need of him out-strengthened my pride. I have never been under the illusion that he loved me, but I would be remiss if I did not admit that I had always hoped his fondness of me would grow as we spent more and more time together. I have forever known that I am a fool and, in truth, I know I have no one to blame save for myself, yet time and again I have opened my heart to his charm only to allow him to destroy it once more. For so many years, I have admonished myself for allowing our relationship to continue in this vein, but my constant reprimands have never taken hold. Even now that he has so brutally and permanently shunned me, the ire I feel only seldom makes an appearance. I know that my anger should at least be equally directed toward us both, but I am unable to share it. Peering through my blight of adoration, I understand that he has always known of my weakness for him and that I have truly been preyed upon. Yet I am ashamed to say that I would weep with joy at the sight of him again. Why can I not accept his final desertion and enjoy release from the constant strikes to my heart? Why will hope not die away and leave me be forever? He has looted me Grandmother, for I do not believe that any other love will find its way into my heart as it has now been rendered blind with nothingness.

Yet in spite of the effect his cruelty has had on me, hope of his return will not exit my heart and I am unable to even conceive the word goodbye. *I miss him so much I cannot fathom the breath I still breathe. I miss everything about him. I miss his face and I miss his voice. I miss the smile he gave only to me and the words he spoke meant for me alone. I miss the music he played and the lyrics he wrote and sang so sweetly. I miss his intelligence and the way he challenged mine. I miss our philosophical discussions and the way our minds complemented each other's. I miss arguing our differing opinions and perspectives. I miss sharing our ideas and our observations of all things amusing. I miss the turn of phrases we were both delighted to share in our playful banter. I miss his jesting when I was perplexed for a riposte and my teasing him for his stubborn contrariness. I miss the way he would look at me when he thought what I said was so ridiculously silly that he could not help his laughter. Now all music is sharp to my ears and I can no longer play. When I think of humorous things, I am impatient to share them with him in the hope of hearing his laughter, but immediately my heart sinks once again as I remember that he has gone, leaving my words unsaid and alone in this world. I lament so terribly all the discussions we will never have, all the laughter will we never share. His departure has left me barren of any laughter at all.*

If you recall, two years ago I learned that he had fallen gravely ill and had taken up residence nearby though never did he contact me. So fearful of this detrimental news, I made my first unsolicited inquiry of him to determine if he was recuperating well. He was happy to hear from me and I learned he was improving daily. We immediately took up our friendship again with lettered communication in which I shortly learned of his living arrangements, a choice of situation he had never before made but was understandable given his health. In short time we were seeing each other at least once every day, if not more. On those rare occasions when we were not face-to-face, a note or two would pass between us to say hello or comment on one thing or another. Most days, he was the only person to whom I spoke and often it would simply be a continuance of our conversation from the day before as if we had not been apart at all. Soon our relationship elevated to new heights that I would never be able to oppose. It grew into something that was greater than ourselves alone, as if it had flourished into its own entity that possessed sentience, and through his words and deeds, I knew that he too felt its significance. In that time, he became the one to whom I told everything, the one to whom I asked everything, the one I trusted and whose opinion I treasured most. He became my best friend. To be deprived of his daily presence more quickly than I can perceive causes me to feel that I have been left utterly alone in this world, for the emptiness that fills my soul is incomprehensible and cannot be explained with mere mortal words. I feel as if my basis of reality has fled and that I am no longer whole.

This is by far the most difficult part of this letter to write, and I am not sure I have the strength to do so, but I will attempt it in the interest of full disclosure nonetheless. During his worldly travels, I knew a man such as he would attract the attention of many women seeking his company, and I have known that he would easily accept their proposals, yet he consistently returned to my patient and pitiable heart. He has always chosen other more sophisticated women for public display, but this time it is different, for the circumstance of his residence has now changed to a permanent familial domestication with the woman he had once called only a companion. She is a countess highborn, and I am only a modest woman without social status and nothing to offer him save for my love. Her husband's death left her with a bright-eyed young boy who Mr. Hawke adores. A gift he has been given to so easily love without restraint. A child who shares his interests and is thirsty for his knowledge. He now has a family. I am ashamed to say that my envy of her remains strong in my heart and my only relief comes when I am able to expel the thought of her from my mind. I have always felt so small and lowly knowing that he never deemed me worthy to permit passage into his world of prestige, but I have never before been ashamed of my simple life. Jealousy of the finery in which he is now sharing with another evermore diminishes my pride as does the dishonor I have placed upon myself for living as only his woman of convenience for so many years. I am even more horrified to admit that one minute I am jealous of the perfection of his life and the love he has found, the love I wish he had for me, and then for an instant the purity of my love for him shines through and I am happy for his deliverance, only to be borne once again to my unforgiving sorrow. I know I am to blame for my own misery, for I have always known that my love for him was unrequited, but each time we spoke my relentless hope to capture his love filled my soul and I could not resist his undivided attention that I had awaited for so long. To finally give his consistent affection to me only to steal it away again is unjustly callous and I feel as though my life has been only an instrument for his mocking eyes. Little did I know that I had in fact sacrificed my dignity further by permitting our friendship to continue over these two years past as his other life progressed, for only after he terminated our relationship did I learn that his "companion" had been his interest for more than a year before he began keeping regular company with me. I know I should be outraged at his deceitful conduct, but I still do not understand, Grandmother, how one can be expected to accept the finality of something one has waited for and dreamt of for so long. It is a brutal request.

Throughout my relationship with Mr. Hawke I have told you that I know my feelings for him are illogical, to say the least. My intellect has been wholly aware of the advantages that would come from the termination of our relationship, but I have not had the courage to attain my salvation with this knowledge. My heart simply would not allow even the slightest attempt. I know I should have never accepted his nonchalant disrespectful treatment of me and I should be thankful for the release I have been afforded by his conclusive departure, for I have experienced all along the staggering consequences of my love for him. In my heart I have always known that someday his preference for another woman would be decisive and that ultimately our attachment would end. I even suspected that it would not end well, but I could never bring myself to confront even the possibility of what I knew as the inevitable. I could never embrace the certainty that one day he would leave me forever. In the last few months of communication, our visits became ever abbreviated until our contact was reduced to only written form, and in each letter his remarks became *increasingly biting until his every word pierced my heart as with a newly sharpened axe. In his comments, I sensed an inner struggle but was bereft of a means to help him for I knew not of its cause. I heard the irritation in his unwarranted and vicious words and in his bitter responses to my opinions and commentaries, none of which I had ever spoken unkindly. Every so often I almost felt as if I was able to ask him of the origination of his animosity, but I was unable to face my suspicion that another may have become more meaningful to him and his continued seeking of my company ever increased his guilt and shame. I simply did not have the strength to release him from the connection of our souls. It grieves me to say that I did not question his change of manner for I was in great fear of losing him, ashamedly fearful of losing this man who for years had treated me with so much selfish intent. Even his hurtful conduct could not persuade me to terminate our friendship. During our last correspondence in which we were discussing an unthreatening subject, he wrote his retort without salutation or valediction and in words so venomous that I was taken aback immediately as if my soul had been impaled. My written response was returned to me boldly marked "unaccepted" in his angry pen, and now my mortification knows no bounds. His summary dismissal and the rage in which he abandoned me have left me flailing in an eddy of utter confusion and my agony grows for I feel as if he now holds only contempt for me. Every day is filled with continual questions that his unspoken word will not ease. He refuses to even confirm his very existence and desperate worry for his continued health plagues my physical being. Nor has he ever once inquired of my welfare, and his lack of consideration tightens my throat with tears. How is it possible that a person has the ability to exhibit such indifference toward another previously called friend? One whose behavior never wavered from kindness? How can another be so callously heartless as to have no consideration for even their friend's well-being? Yet this feeling of earned indignation gives way to my mourning, and the image of him in his new life leaves me grief-stricken once more as my mind envisions the one he chose joyful at receiving his sudden undistracted attention and the additional time vacated by our communication. It causes me to visualize the all-consuming affection we* shared now being rained upon another in their coupled life. How jealous I am that she is the only one fortunate to be favored with his wit and intelligence, to feel the touch of his hand. When my thoughts veer in that direction, it sickens my soul and perpetrates an illness that brings me to my knees. He cannot fathom what he has done to me and, more cruelly, he does not care.

I know that his choice is best for him, and in my finest moments, I am at peace to know he has found what he needs in this life. It pacifies me to know that being a father has finally lent him the ability to offer another soul pure generosity expecting nothing in return. When grace visits my heart, I am glad he has now absorbed himself in the beautiful life that is there for him in his family. In my purest moments, I want only peace in his heart and love in his life, but altruism quickly exits my spirit and relinquishes itself to my desperate need of him. What is one to do with unfinished affection? For without his friendship, I have no thought of tomorrow and it feels as though my debilitation has deemed me unworthy of any future. I have lost my way Grandmother, and I am missing the person I had once been. How have I become so unimportant in my own life? Is there any worth to be found in my plight? Have all these tormenting years been for naught? Could it be that I was meant only to perform a minor role in his life and my part has been fulfilled? Or that perhaps, as my only solace, grace has mercifully been bestowed upon us and the role I have played was meant to deliver both our souls to a greater capacity for kindness? Purpose or no, the cost is too high Grandmother, and my shattered heart rails at its injustice. Many times I have wished never to have met him for all the pain he has caused me, but I am unable to find the truth in my desire. I have allowed my dignity to plummet so deeply that I cannot entertain the thought of anger toward him and, against all rationality, even feel as though it would be a betrayal. My honor has been damaged so by my loyalty to him that I still cannot summon words to slight him in any way. In the past, my confidants have asked me why I hold no anger for his nonchalant treatment of me and are befuddled at my reply that I am incapable. They have continually advised that it is my right, and I have always known the truth in their words, but I still falter in my capacity to claim it. I suspect anger would finally unearth my ability to acknowledge all the characteristics of his I found distasteful, those objectionable traits that were always over-shadowed by my need for him, those failings that I would not admit due to my love of his better qualities. Yet there are times, though seldom, when I glimpse a minute occurrence of resentment and I appreciate the notion that if he has truly eternalized his silence this time, my heart will have seen the last of its devastation and the belief in my worth will return to forever stake its claim on my soul. How I long for that liberation to come, for it has been three months since his last missive and I still awaken each morning thinking I will see him, only for my soul to collapse again at the knowledge that I will not. There is nothing that I would not give for this agony to cease.

   Forgive me Grandmother, for this outpouring has left me bereft of all energy and so I must conclude my writing for now to take to rest once more.

~~~~~~~~~~~~~~~~~~~~~~~~~~~~~~~~~

July 23

Grandmother,

It is morning, and I have once again awakened from sleep with excited anticipation of what Mr. Hawke and I will speak of today only to be violently pitched once more by the memory of my loss. When I began this letter last night, I had no idea how much my soul needed to speak or how much it had to say. Just knowing that you will be reading my words, I believe that perhaps my assessment of my situation has begun to shift. Again this morning, after realization of his abandonment, the familiar heavy sadness filled my heart and I was without the will to rise from my dark and comforting bed so I closed my eyes once more to capture release of blessed sleep. When I awoke, I was in the trance of a dream that was so jarring my sadness did not make its usual initial appearance as the dream took my heart in a different direction. I dreamt that I met me face-to-face. I saw a woman stretching to peer over a fence beyond which I achieved only a glimpse, and when she turned away from me to go, she tried to hide by ducking below my windowpane. She moved quickly in an attempt to escape my sight, but my surprised suspicion of her identity made me call to her my own name. Being caught, my other self proudly and righteously straightened her stance and looked me square in the eye with angry face. I then saw my double clearly and recognized the woman I had once known, pride in her countenance. She did not wait for my inquiry but immediately chastised me for condemning myself to this life of desolation and for ignoring my true self, the person I have lost, and the pleasures I have missed each day that I have spent in my misery. She was angry with me for not appreciating the time that I have been given and for leaving stagnant the occupational skills I have developed which have always before delighted and inspired me to rise from my bed. Was she telling me that I have allowed enough of this nonsense? That it is time to finally continue on my journey in this life? Could it be that I am healing? As I write this letter, I am thankful that my words have returned to me to be delivered upon parchment once more. And as these words unfold, the sun is rising and hope has made its tentative inquiry into my heart, for I am finally happy to see its brilliance. Its appearance instills a long-awaited wish to even desire its warmth upon my face again and excites my memory of the exhilaration I find each time I take to the fields on horseback. The joy of anticipation touches my heart, and this time I trust its promise to grow there. I am so happy with the lightness of my soul that I am impatient to ready myself for an outing. Please forgive the break in this letter once more and I promise its conclusion upon my return.

~~~~~~~~~~~~~~~~~~~~~~~~~~~~~

Alas Grandmother, I am finishing this missive much sooner than I expected. As I donned my coat to ready myself for my excursion, I felt the long sought eagerness for the walk to the stables and began to remind myself of the location of my friend's tack and all that I would need to ready him for our venture. Reaching for my riding gloves, I glanced out into the day only to find that the sky had turned back to grey. The sun's infusion of hope had fooled me, for I saw it had only peered through a window of clouds for a mere moment and I am distraught at its unkind teasing. My heart has delved once more into its immobilizing depression and I have returned my lonely coat and gloves to their long-occupied place in my armoire.

It is that I seek your understanding and your wisdom Grandmother, in closing this letter, for I do not know how much longer I am able to awaken each day in which every thought injures my spirit and only the slightest of tethers secures my soul.

Forever your loving Granddaughter

~~~~~~

5 August

My darling Granddaughter,

I am grateful to have received your post of 22 July and pray that my dispatch to you will follow in its successful voyage. What a pleasure it is to hear from you, for I have missed your letters, yet it is with great sadness that I read your words. I lament the disagreeable distance that separates us, but am pleased you have turned to me to express your grief. Please know that I am securing immediate arrangements to be by your side and will be making my way to you as soon as the next ship sails. But until the time we are together, I pray this missive will help soothe you, for I can feel by the distress in the words you have penned that your spirit is in a state of great fragility. Please know that my only wish is to hold you in my arms and properly express my sorrow for your suffering, but until that time is possible, I ask that you letter to me your self-discoveries as you journey through your heart's tribulation, for I am in need to know of your welfare.

Before I begin to convey my thoughts regarding the events that have transpired, I want you to know that I am of the opinion that Mr. Hawke's treatment of you is inexcusably deplorable and that your torment is well founded. It is in fact my wish to have the good fortune to articulate to him exactly what crime he has committed and that he should be greatly ashamed of his behavior. Nevertheless, I ask you to understand that any observations I express are not intended to devalue the devastation you are experiencing, but perhaps my thoughts will ease your pain and allow you a new appreciation for the role you played in his life and, much more importantly, your own, for understanding your actions as well as his is one of the keys that will gain your freedom.

I have not been a subscriber to the thought that "time heals all wounds," for it has been my experience that, though time allows our wounds to subside, their effect remains in one form or another. *In* order to benefit from lessons we have been offered, we must progress at our own pace through the contemplation of what each element of grief means to us. *Do* not be mistaken in believing your plight has no worth, for from the finality of your long-time struggle you will continue to learn much about yourself. *Living* through the loss of a love so strong is one of the most difficult things we can do, yet one of the most empowering as well. *There* are those whom feel that they have no need to extract meaning from the challenges they face in their lives, but that is not my position. *I* believe that exploring experiences to their fullest adds a profound richness to life that would otherwise be relinquished. *Undergoing* a loss is no exception, though it is much more difficult to examine than the experiences of lesser significance. *Though* a wound may heal completely, the scar it leaves is as deep as the loss itself, but, if we impart our proper attention, it can serve to remind us of our victorious transition through all the phases of grief. *Perhaps* our lesson is to realize and accept that just as genuine love is never fully exorcised, neither is genuine pain. *Each* is its own blessing, and one cannot be entirely appreciated without the other. *The* art is to learn how to carry both with graceful wisdom. *That* is the strength and confidence we gain by experiencing a loss to its fullest. *Through* our victory, we earn empowerment. *Grief* must make its own progression and survival requires one to fully experience each phase before advancing to the next. *If* one attempts to avoid any stage, he or she will stay tightly fastened to one element or another and full relief will not transpire. *Without* allowing grief to run its natural course from beginning to end, peace will never be found in the heart and the soul will stay imprisoned forever.

I understand the immobility of which you speak, for when we first learn that we have lost someone dear to us, shock renders our mind capable of only disbelief. *We* cannot appreciate the truth of the occurrence and can only judge *it as a fallacy. We hope that the news has been miscommunicated or misheard and that it has been only a horrible mistake. The loss of a love that occurs as suddenly as yours has the capability to stagger even our walk for we have no time to prepare our hearts for its acceptance. The hope of its reversal strikes us and can remain in the soul for what seems like time interminable. The amount of time it takes for any one heart to heal is different from all the rest and cannot be rushed. Hope will not subside until it is ready, and in truth, one should not request it vacate the soul altogether for the destruction of its potential will void the soul completely and the heart will forever be closed. A life without hope is a life of sorrow and until hope is ready to surrender to the finality of a situation, it cannot proceed to its next purpose. If you allow hope to take the time it needs to subside, its conclusion will allow you to reconsider the blame you have placed upon yourself for the misery you are now experiencing and freedom of heart will begin its journey toward you. Releasing hope for Mr. Hawke's return, and the burden it carries, will permit you to be comforted by knowing that you have never veered from your kindness toward him and have done nothing to deserve his unfounded ostracism.*

Although I view the fact that he reactivated his communication with you while in a relationship with another as notably unscrupulous and horrifically unjust to you, only he can determine the validity of others' opinions just as only you can determine those directed toward you. Chastising yourself for acting the fool will only prolong your despondency, for the heart of a love so vast lends no ear to reason but only hears its own passionate need and must be executed to whatever conclusion it requires. If others deem you a fool or otherwise cast judgment, please do not take it to heart, for only you know the extent of your love. I understand your embarrassment in feeling that others view you as weak-willed, but your emotions are valid and belong to you alone. Any discomfiture caused by his or her opinion is undeserved for there is nothing in love that is pitiable. All pain, no matter what manner it takes, must be allowed the time needed to recede. *I* know, darling, that while it incessantly grips your heart you feel as if nothing else exists. *Others* may discount it as foolhardy and a waste of precious time, but it must be navigated thoroughly to lessen the burden of the weight you carry. *Some* may undervalue or otherwise appraise your situation, but *I* know the torment you continue to suffer is genuine, and *I* know its depth twins the grandeur of the love you still carry for your *Mr. Hawke*. *I* understand the excruciating agony in which you are living, for wounds need care, and damage to a heart is no exception. *It* too requires attention to be healed. *I* have learned that pain must be witnessed, for that is the only means by which it will be exorcised, and without escape, anguish will not relinquish its hold to facilitate the next phase that grief must take toward its alleviation. *To* begin grief's process, each particular element of pain must be heard and acknowledged by another, for without that validation, pain continues to burrow into the soul with unrelenting obstinacy and will not cease for even a moment. *Another* person must bear witness and appreciate the reality of your suffering and the true physicality of your despair without judgment or advice, for your pain is as powerful as your love and the agony of a loss so great cannot simply be wished away. *I* understand that even your closest confidants my not possess the ability to recognize that you are in need of someone to simply listen to your recount of every awful word he has uttered and every deplorable action he has taken. *When* they only inquire if you have turned your attention to other matters and left *Mr. Hawke* in the past, they do not fathom that their inquiry simply devalues your pain. *I* wish to convey to you, my dearest, my appreciation for the fact that a love unreturned can still be the most profound of your life and *I* understand the empty loneliness of a broken heart when the company of that love has been stripped away leaving even sleep unable to grant release of the heart's agony. *The* loss of a love so immeasurable is very much a death, and can be even more traumatic than the physical death of a loved one. *Though* we miss our departed with all our hearts, we may rely on our faith that they have moved on to their next destination. *We* gather together to honor our loss and comfort each other's kindred sorrow, but often in the death of a love we are left behind in a cloud of unknowing. This, especially when coupled with an element of undefined rejection, incites the pain of a loss to stab at the heart without cessation. In the death of a love, we are alone. For you, my dear child, the impetus of your pain is ever encouraged by thoughts of the manner in which he now spends his days and their insistence only adds more oppression to your already over-burdened spirit. That particular source of pain, as well as all the others, must travel the avenues it requires for one's soul to gain release from its ever-powerful grip, for the heart must navigate through all emotions it needs and, in some circumstances, jealousy can play its role.

Some say that jealousy and anger are sinful without exception, but I disagree. When jealousy is moderated, it can serve as an entrance to anger and our offender's objectionable characteristics to which we are otherwise blind come into view to afford us the ability to perceive the situation in its entirety, and in that full depiction, lies the road to solace. I believe that the constructive expression of anger is a necessary step that grief must follow, for with anger we open our hearts and minds to the realities we would not otherwise entertain while in the throes of adoration. Consider that the jealousy you sometimes feel of his perfect life, though understandable, is actually unwarranted, for the image of perfection one creates in his or her mind is never a reality. As much as some would debate the truth, perfection does not exist. The new life you envision him living is certainly not as perfect as you imagine, for just as every person has his or her deficiencies, every situation has its own. The sense of losing your dignity by the inability to anger is understandable, but by missing your honor, you have proven its existence. The strength of your loyalty to him has merely hidden it from sight, and you will find it again. I understand that releasing a fidelity so long held, even one so highly undeserved, can prove to be a monumental feat, but I also believe that it is worth the struggle, for upon its liberation you will return that commitment to yourself. You are correct to believe that anger at Mr. Hawke for his deplorable treatment of you is your right and you will come to find that your belief will play a large measure in your salvation. Allowing anger its voice is not only valid but also necessary and should be viewed not as a betrayal of loyalty but as a fundamental element in a worthwhile relationship. Someday clarity will visit your mind and you will come to see Mr. Hawke's faults plainly. Among other imperfections, I am sure you will realize that he had not the capability or the courage to end your relationship well with honesty and compassion, and it will help you become aware that his strength of character was not, in the end, what you always thought it to be. You will know when the time has come to allow yourself to ruminate on his each and every flaw, and when you are ready to exclaim your criticisms, speak them vigorously to free your heart from their poison. The release of anger facilitates acceptance of the finality of a situation and it is my belief that acceptance is the most difficult phase of grief that must be conquered, as well as the most imperative. The acceptance of any loss is hard-won, and a loss without understanding the cause for its occurrence is the most trying of all. In a death, the reasons are clear, but the loss of a love oftentimes does not provide those explanations and one must rely on speculation alone. Acceptance is a monumental task and takes much time and honesty with oneself for it to be truly surmounted.

Please darling, read my next words only when you feel you are ready, only when you feel your heart is willing to contemplate what I wish to serve as guidance in your healing. Read them only when your soul has had enough time to regain a sense of mobility. These are only suggestions and may be difficult to attend, but I write them in an attempt to help you assess your role, as well as Mr. Hawke's, in the events that have occurred and I believe at some juncture they must be considered in their entirety. These are ideas that I know you are already aware but must be brought into full light, for only through understanding may we continue our progression through the corridors in which grief must travel. Sometimes questions are more important than *solutions, for even though we may think we know the answers, we still should ask why. It is only by our contemplation do we discover more of ourselves and by doing so relieve our minds of any unwarranted culpability for the tragedy that has occurred. Know clearly that I do not offer a single excuse for Mr. Hawke's malicious treatment of you or for so selfishly taking advantage of your kind and selfless heart for so long, but I hope your rumination of these possibilities will assist in your complete recovery.*

I understand the devastation that brutal words spoken to an open heart renders, but blind to us are the explanations for how one gains the capacity for malevolence. I have come to learn that one can never truly understand the motivations for another's actions and that the reason may be unknown to even the one who exhibits the behavior. We cannot know what experiences have determined how another manages the events that occur in his or her life, we can only attempt to interpret them with as much understanding and compassion our own experiences have taught us. Since Mr. Hawke has refused to provide you with an explanation for his behavior, I can only suggest conjectures and suppositions. The fact is, most probably you will never know what caused him to treat you so poorly and will be forever disconcerted as to why he directed such sudden anger toward you or as to why he so brutally rejected your last missive. However, if you try to glean education from your experience, your ability for compassion will strengthen and you may find that you will be able to put it to good use for yourself as well as others.

I offer to you the thought that the gravity of your Mr. Hawke's illness may have instigated a different perspective on his life and, as time transpired, he progressively acknowledged his gratitude toward his companion for the care she had continually provided and that recognition became a genuine love for her. At the same time, his role as a father matured and he increasingly discovered the joy of selflessness that being a parent provides and that, in turn, became a love for the boy as well as for his family unit as a whole. I have no doubt that his fondness for you was genuine, but perhaps during those last few months of communication what you witnessed in his bitter words and behavior was his struggle with the profound change that had occurred in his life as well as the guilt he was experiencing for enjoying the company of both you and his family simultaneously. It could be that the conflict you sensed in him evidenced the fight with his habit of you. When his shame built to an insufferable height, the difference of opinion in your last correspondence afforded him the luxury of stealing the excuse to cut off all communication. It is the human condition to be resistant to change, and his deplorable behavior toward you may have exhibited his inner battle with the choice he had never before needed to make. As such, to relieve himself of his combat, he eliminated you from his life with a disdainful stroke of his pen. Perhaps your Mr. Hawke had not the insight to recognize that this conflict was the origination of his cruelty and that the anger he was exhibiting was in truth directed toward himself. In lieu of this knowledge, he leveled his acrimony upon you instead, for only by the exorcism of his anger in some fashion could he assuage his guilt. I do believe that your Mr. Hawke felt the intensity of your bond as well as you, and he may or may not be aware of the suffering he has inflicted upon you, but perhaps he does not possess the strength to allow himself to admit that he is capable of such brutality, let alone offer you an explanation, and so refuses further contact. Perhaps it is even so that he has yet to learn the value of compassion. Nevertheless, the lack of his ability to recognize his vicious behavior and tender an apology to you is quite unforgivable and is another shortcoming for which he should be utterly ashamed.

As for deriving meaning from your role in the relationship, it is possible that Mr. Hawke was having difficulty accepting that the exciting life he had enjoyed for so long was gone forever and you, being the last vestige of that life, helped him cross the bridge between the old life his illness now prohibits into the new, more sedentary life he is living. To be given the task to survive the pain of such an immense sacrifice may feel unmerited and much too heavy a burden, but you, my dearest, are among the very few that have the strength to carry such a weight. More importantly than any explanation for Mr. Hawke's behavior I have offered, I want you to contemplate the idea that the foremost purpose of your struggle is not to assist him in finding his way through the change that has occurred in his life, but that its true purpose is to finally achieve your own happiness, for through his wretched behavior, though unintentionally, he has also set you free of any further pain he would no doubt have caused you. Consider the idea that, even if your relationship had become public at any time throughout the years, the fact he is capable of such cruelty and deceit would have most likely demanded a destructive end for you. You are deserving of a joyful life filled with love, and as long as your unrequited dedication to him remains, the possibility for you to achieve it is tenuous at best.

I know that the situation in which you have been abandoned seems terribly cruel but consider that, for a while, your wish was granted and you have now experienced the meaningful relationship with Mr. Hawke that you always desired. For that time, he chose your company above others and, though some form of your love for him may remain, perhaps you will come to view his cruelty as the means by which you have been afforded the acceptance you need to grieve the loss of your love instead of remaining forever in the torment of his blindness to your worth. You have suffered that existence for far too long, and without its end it will continue to keep your spirit imprisoned and your heart will have no hope of liberation. Consider that you have, in truth, been given the opportunity to love again. It may be that your relationship with Mr. Hawke has achieved its purpose and each of you have been given the opportunity to understand the teaching's significance to you as individuals. Experience can be a brutal instructor, and it is not your charge to ponder if he is capable of putting to good use the opportunity that has been afforded, but you have the fortune to choose to do so. Perhaps your lesson is to understand that your life is meant for many things and that it is time for you to progress to the next. We cannot know what our unique destinies entail and the labyrinth of tests we must endure to become our finest selves may feel unfairly daunting and impossible. The depth of the pain you feel now has been rendered by the happiness you felt while your relationship existed, for love and pain are testaments to each other and one cannot exist without the other. That, darling, is the cost of loving. The expense of your aid to Mr. Hawke may seem unendurably high, but someday you will know that your time with him has not been in vain for you will appreciate that loving him in spite of the pain he has caused you is a divine gift. Sustaining kindness toward one's transgressor after such vicious behavior without retention of pain, anger, jealousy and the *feeling of injustice is an extremely difficult feat but will be highly compensated. Though we may feel our offender is unworthy of our pardon, it is only through forgiveness that we release our souls from pain completely. The arduous road to forgiveness is long and taxing, but it must be bravely travelled, for the more difficult the journey, the more precious the reward. Forgiveness is an art that is only attained by placing ourselves in the position of another's heart, and though you may feel it is ever distant, mastering forgiveness is the gateway to the ultimate blessing of original love and its liberation. You will understand that the survival of your loss will prove to be grace delivered upon you, for when it manifests itself into your immense ability for compassion toward others its strength will be as equally powerful as the severity of your tribulation. The sacrifice you made will become increasingly more valuable when others in need follow, for you will have gained the ability to be of great assistance, a gift only those of high caliber are granted, and when you are warmed by the gratitude from others for your benevolence, the feeling of inadequacy for your station in life will be replaced by quiet contentment. In the course of healing, your final freedom will surface when your will to remember overcomes your will to forget and your desire for Mr. Hawke's friendship will be replaced by the desire for his happiness. Upon that day, you will have achieved the ability to forgive and when you think of him an elegant reminiscence of your love, and even your loss, will replace pain's burden and only love will shine through. The peace you have earned by conquering your grief will cause you a gentle serenity when you think of him living his chosen life as well as when you remember the one you had together. And though your actions will never be witnessed by him, you may choose to believe that you have helped him proceed into the life that was meant for him to live and that your genuine hope for his peace of mind has found its way into his soul and has lightened any burden his heart may have carried for his part in your friendship as well as its cruel termination. Your battle surmounted will prove that you are one of the rare souls who have the courage to risk your heart by revealing your soul unreservedly, and it will attest to the fact that you possess the ability to give all of yourself to another for the time you are allowed. I know darling that someday your love for him will achieve its unconditional destiny and that your soul will find its way back to its purest form, for you will have learned that you are capable of forsaking your happiness for that of another without forsaking yourself. When you discover this as your truth, Granddaughter, your broken heart will be restored and you will find your peace. It is then that you will lay claim to your true self once more.*

I know that these words do not relieve the anguish you feel at this moment, but perhaps your rumination of them will further your quest toward the liberation of your laden heart. They are meant to offer hope, and I understand that in the beginning when the shock of your loss has yet to subside and the hardship of living without your love feels as if it is too difficult to bear, the road to freedom of soul seems never-ending. All you can do is remember to lift your eyes, for your head will always follow. And now that you have begun again, continue your writing, for the gift of your creativity will allow your pain to become a story instead of a life. Remember to keep your faith in the power of the spirit you have been given and that your call will be heard. I read in your words the beginning of your soul's journey back to you, and I ask that, even though its appearance is fleeting, please believe that it is indeed making its first tentative steps toward returning your heart to its freedom. But until that time, know that there is a place for your broken heart and that I am holding it for you until your courage heals your soul well enough to reclaim it. Know that I am hearing your tears in the night and feeling them in the day. And when your devastation comes to feel as if living without him will destroy you completely, close your eyes and feel my hand upon your brow and my love rocking you to sleep.

I pray, my dearest girl, that my words will help sooth your plight and that they will find their way to you as swiftly as the skylark flies.

My every thought is with you,
Your loving Grandmother

Wisdom

Transforms

Challenges

Into

Opportunities

AUTHOR BIOGRAPHY

Kelly Hamilton was born and raised in the wine country of Northern California and continues to call it home. Growing up surrounded by the stunning beauty of the San Francisco Bay area, she has developed a unique style in expressing gratitude for the quiet blessings that envelope us all. Her introspection offers us a distinctive appreciation for the value of all emotions and how they can be repurposed to develop a better understanding of ourselves. Kelly always encourages readers to write and she welcomes your questions and comments at GhostTracksTome@Yahoo.com.

Printed in the United States
By Bookmasters